MW01601323

THE BLIND BLOGGER'S FIRST SPEAKING AND SIGNING ADVENTURES

.

+ HOW YOU CAN CONQUER YOUR FEARS

MAXWELL IVEY, JR.

The Blind Blogger's First Speaking and Signing Adventures (+ How You Can Conquer Your Fears)

Copyright © 2020 by Maxwell Ivey Jr.

ISBN-13: 978-1-7354286-1-1

Cover creation courtesy of Ravi Verma from rdezines

Editing and formatting courtesy of Lorraine Reguly from https://wordingwell.com

Dedication

This book is dedicated to anyone who has
fears and to conquering those fears.

Table of Contents

MAXWELL IVEY JR.

Foreword

Hello! I'm known as Super Joe Pardo and I was both touched and honored when I was asked to write the foreword for this particular book. I am a perfect example of someone who embodies the lessons Max teaches others—lessons he will also teach you!

In 2015, Maxwell Ivey reached out to me, via email. I didn't know him, but after being inspired by the experiences that he talked about (how is an ex-carnie who was now a blogger and podcaster), I agreed to have him as a guest on my podcast.

Back then, I was a little over a year into running my show, the Dreamers Podcast. I recall being excited because I didn't get many emails from people who wanted to be on the show at the time (although that would change in 2016)!

Having Max on the Dreamers Podcast was a memorable moment in my show's history.

He made me feel comfortable with his friendly approach and openness to his blindness. We hit it off immediately. We also exchanged several emails after that and during 2016, which led to me sending out an email in early 2017, about hosting another anniversary party for my show.

Max reached out to me, asking if he could come, because he felt he would be the perfect speaker for the event. I was touched by his intention to travel across the country by train, all the way from Texas to South Jersey (right outside of Philadelphia, Pennsylvania) by himself. That blew me away.

I immediately said, "YES!"

When Max arrived at the train station, he was much later than expected, and I'm sure you'll read about that in the pages that follow. He took a cab from the 30th Street Station in Philadelphia to North Camden, New Jersey, where I worked at the time, and arrived at around 5:15 PM. I remember thinking the cab driver must have thought he was crazy—a blind, white guy heading to North Camden, as the sun was setting. That is Max, though, doing things you might not expect and making everyone around him feel comfortable in the process.

Max and I went out for dinner at the Applebee's down the street from the Holiday Inn. I will never forget the conversation that we had while we were there in that booth. Max told me how comfortable I made him feel. The feeling was mutual. He talked about how he was self-conscious about

10

eating in front of other people. I told Max about how much he had taught me in that short period of time we had been together—including a major lesson in patience, which is something I have always worked hard to try and have more of, but also something with which I have always struggled.

Helping Max navigate the world by giving him my shoulder was a totally new thing to me. Up until then, I had not been around anyone who was blind.

The next morning, I picked him up and took him back to North Camden to speak at my workplace, HopeWorks. He delivered an impactful message and had many youths sticking around to chat with him afterward.

The next day was the DreamCon event, where Max delivered the opening speech and completely knocked it out of the park. Speakers throughout the rest of the day referenced him and his talk because it was that impactful. I can honestly say I never had any doubt that he would be so impactful and make so many friends from that event. I learned so much from him during the time I spent with him that long weekend in 2017. Little did I know that it was the beginning of what would become a stronger and stronger relationship!

As the years have gone by, I have watched Max grow into a more confident speaker and person. We now talk almost weekly and help each other, whenever possible. Max has spoken at several of my events since then and I am always excited when he wants to be a part of them. It is an honor to be able to call him a friend. He has delivered many great pieces of knowledge and insight into my work, which have really made a difference in my journey.

As you read through the pages of this book, remember that you are on a journey—even if you don't realize it. Max's story will inspire you to take risks and be more honest with yourself and others. Learning how to start by asking for help can lead you down a path that neither you nor the person who helps you may expect. You need to be willing to do things that move the needle.

Over the years, my journey has crossed paths with many people I can now call friends because they were willing to do things that pushed past their self-imposed limitations. Max is one of those people, and after you finish reading through this book, you simply have to reach out to him. You never know what adventure you will be inspired to take on next in your life!

Chapter 1: Where the Idea Came From

Hi! My name is Max, and I am a totally blind gentleman from Conroe, Texas, USA. I am an entrepreneur, author, motivational speaker, coach, podcaster, and an online media publicist. I am also internationally known as The Blind Blogger.

This book is a chronicle of my first speaking and signing events.

I write my books in a friendly, conversational style. I like to share my experiences like I'm writing about them to a close, personal friend. I put my thoughts and feelings down while events are happening, in hopes that my honesty and openness will encourage you to share your own story with the world.

The one thing I've learned over the years is you should not wait until you think your story is good enough before you start sharing it. In this case, I wrote about my first tour. During that trip, I had my first public-speaking gig as well as my first book signing. After a conversation with my friend and editor, Lorraine Reguly, it was decided that not only was it a great idea, but it could also be the beginning of a series of books about my

13

many firsts. I'm hoping that sharing my experiences will encourage you not to wait to start living your own journey.

It all started when we were kicking around title ideas for my third book about my Amtrak adventure to New York City. She understands my love for the train and its slower, more leisurely way of getting from Point A to Point B. She said that as long as I was going to be taking the train, maybe the book about my New York City trip should be called *My First Amtrak Adventure*. That lead to a conversation about writing books on the subjects of my first speaking tour, my first book tour, and—maybe someday—my first documentary film or first world tour.

One of the possible titles was *The Blind Blogger's First Amtrak Adventure: What Can Happen When You Live Life as If No One Is Watching.* After getting feedback from others, we decided upon calling my third book (the first one in my travel series) *The Blind Blogger's NYC Adventures (+ How You Can Make Your Dreams Come True).*

Exchanges like these are why you should have a really good editor.

Lorraine is my editor and also my friend.

Shortly after meeting me, she interviewed me. She was curious about how I function on a day-to-day basis as a blind person.

14

Through our many email exchanges and phone conversations, we developed a bond. I even hired her to help me with different visual tasks I had to do online (on my websites and my social media profiles). She edited some of my blog posts, too.

Lorraine also made me see the value in writing properly, in my social media posts as well as in the newsletters or emails, using the standard conventions that I ignored or didn't care about, so she was the natural choice to edit my first book, *Leading You Out of the Darkness into the Light: A Blind Man's Inspirational Guide to Success*.

I hired her to format both versions of it, too.

Because she did such a great job, I enlisted her editing and author assistant services again with my second book, *It's Not the Cookie, It's the Bag: An Easy-to-Follow Guide for Weight Loss Success*, and my third book, *The Blind Blogger's NYC Adventures*.

Naturally, I chose her to help me publish this book, too. I hope you enjoy reading it as much as I enjoyed writing it! I also hope it inspires you to write about your experiences!

Key Takeaways:

You should not wait until you think your story is good enough before you start sharing it!

A great editor can help you make your story shine, come alive, and transport the reader into your world!

Chapter 2: How the Tour Came to Be

I know a lot of people talk about the Law of Attraction and manifesting their dreams.

If you know anything about me, then you know I firmly believe that you have to ask for what you want and need. You can do that through praying, meditating, using a vision board, sending emails, making phone calls, talking to someone about your day or your experiences, etc.

I had a desire to share my story with even more people. I had appeared on lots of podcasts and radio shows, and the hosts always spoke of how inspiring my story was. I felt like I could inspire even more people in person, or affect them in a way not possible through online interviews. My friends also suggested that I would make a great motivational speaker, so I sent out lots of emails to local groups that might have a need for a guest speaker. I sent pitch emails to various places I could find online. I filled out submission forms. I joined websites that match event organizers with available speakers.

Despite doing all that, I had nothing to show for my efforts.

Then, one day, I received an email from Super Joe Pardo, host of the *Dreamers Podcast*. I had appeared on Joe's show over a year earlier, and he had been impressed by me. He was announcing a new motivational conference called DreamCon. He was reaching out to past guests to see if they would be interested in coming to Swedesboro, New Jersey, near Philadelphia, to share their stories with the attendees. It would be his first ever event for fellow Dreamers, but he had done the Mid-Atlantic Podcast Conference for three years, so he had experience in the field. I felt that he would have a good chance of delivering a solid audience by drawing from his past successes. I also felt it meant he knew about setting prices, promotion, and organization.

I replied to the email, telling him that I would love to attend and could give a talk on the subject of fear with a talk called "Just Press Send—Don't Let Your Fear Keep You from Your Destiny." He replied immediately, saying he would love to have me.

Now, this is another case where I acted without thinking about it too much. I gave no consideration to could he pay, what I would wear, how would I get there, where I would stay, or if the other speakers would like me. I just said to myself, *Yes, I can do this. More importantly, I want to do this.* I asked Joe if he could help with any of the expenses. He said with it being the first annual event—and a reasonably priced one—that he could not.

I didn't back out. I knew, somehow, I would find a way to go. Just like I somehow found a way to go to New York, I felt I would find a way to do this, too. So, I started working toward going.

The first thing I did was to start telling people I was going. Even though I had doubts, I didn't allow fear to come into how I was sharing the news. I added that I would love to find other events to attend. I also mentioned that it would be great to have friends to stay with along the way.

I had previously posted to my email list and to some Facebook groups. I asked people if they would be willing to host me. I was really surprised (although I probably shouldn't have been) when many of my friends and connections said that they would open up their homes to me.

After I announced the trip to Philadelphia, a friend named Al Chase invited me to come to Buffalo after DreamCon. He said I could stay with him and his girlfriend. He also said he could get me some bookings for public talks or book signings. Following that, my friend, Ashley Coleman, invited me to come give a talk to the students at the Governor Morehead School for the Blind in Raleigh, North Carolina.

I then had some great email exchanges with a lady in Columbia, South Carolina, named Katie. She ended up buying a park train I was selling via the Midway Marketplace (my amusement equipment brokering business). We talked about my coming to visit her and her agritourism business. She mentioned showing me her Lipizzaner stallions. She said she was just finishing building an arena for horse shows and other outdoor events. I told her that I was now doing public speaking as the Blind Blogger, and she said perhaps the arena would be done in time for me to break it in. Either way, I could do a story on her farm for the Midway Marketplace website.

Then, I thought, *Why not finish it up with a visit to upstate South Carolina and see some of my dad's side of the family for the first time in many years?*

As I began planning my itinerary, I realized that I would have a six-week trip where I would only be staying in hotels for one weekend!

I think that is a perfect example of finding solutions instead of making excuses.

Who says that an author or speaker has to pay all of their own expenses? Who says you have to charge huge fees to be able to afford to travel? And who says you have to stay in hotels or motels while you are on the road?

It may just be because I'm blind, but I can see some definite advantages of doing it the way I did it. It allowed other people to be part of my story and my success. When it came to money, it took a lot of the strain off of me. It also meant that I got some help from locals when it came to approaching bookstores, booking meeting rooms, or reserving event venues. Heck, they even helped me with gaining attention from local media! They might even help me with getting better rates, once I am ready to start buying advertising.

There is a myth that to be a successful public speaker, you have to do all the work yourself, pay all the bills, stay in fancy hotels, take airplanes, have an extravagant wardrobe, and as a result, have a huge budget. I still have problems where it comes to money and an attitude *of lack* rather than *abundance*, but I'm getting better. When I left for my New York City adventures, I had $420 on me. This time, I had an even $500, but I had to pay my transportation costs to the Amtrak station in Houston out of that… and I had some money problems along the way.

Don't worry, I'm still the straight shooter I've always been. I'm going to tell you about those times and how I dealt with them. I'll share what happened when events fell through, when people didn't show up, and when I ran short of money. I will share these things partly to show you that you can still reach your goals despite having hardships along the way, and also to remind myself that I can survive such setbacks and thrive through them.

I'm hoping that my experiences will encourage you to take a big risk in your own life and get out there. I want you to do it before you are ready—because none of us are ever ready.

I started by taking one step. I replied to Joe's email and said, "Yes, I want to do this."

In doing that, I was also saying to myself, *I believe I am ready to do this, whether I am or not.* Most importantly, I was saying, *I deserve to have this opportunity.*

I hope you will enjoy following along as I share my first speaking trip that also included my first book signing. The whole trip was a great learning experience for me.

Key Takeaways:

Seize opportunities when they come your way!

Instead of making excuses, focus on finding solutions!

Use your resources to reach out for help.

Let other people be part of your story and your success!

Chapter 3: My Tour Approach

After I made the decision to go on a six-week speaking tour to share my message with others and gain more exposure for my books, I planned on enjoying myself by doing some fun stuff along the way, like visiting Niagara Falls, having lunch in Times Square, petting some Lipizzaner horses, and visiting family I hadn't seen in years.

My itinerary consisted of heading to Swedesboro, New Jersey, to give a talk to the students at HopeWorks (a non-profit organization that helps youth who are "at risk") and then another talk to the attendees of the inspirational conference called DreamCon. From there, I'd go to Niagara Falls, Ontario, Canada. After that, I'd go to Buffalo, New York, to address more youth from a group called Young People with a Purpose. I wanted to give another talk to the football players and staff of the Buffalo Gladiators. I'd then move on to Raleigh, North Carolina, to speak with the students and their families at the Governor Morehead School for the Blind. Following that, I'd go to Columbia, South Carolina, to check in with the proposed buyer of a park train, Katie, who was also the lady with the prized

Lipizzaner stallions. I figured it would be fun and also give me a great post for my other site, the Midway Marketplace.

Next, I planned to head to Union and Jonesville, South Carolina, by way of Spartanburg, to meet the Ivey side of my family, whom I hadn't seen in person since I lost a lot of weight and got healthy. Along the way, I planned to continue booking additional speaking and book-signing gigs.

But before I tell you the story of what happened (and didn't happen, because a few plans fell through) during this trip, I want to tell you how everything all got started, because I'm all about asking for things.

When I was frustrated with the negative responses to my attempts to book events for our small carnival, my dad used to tell me, "Max, if you don't ask, they can't say yes." He would then say something to make me laugh, and I'd make the next call. So, I am always asking, whether it's sending pitch emails, meditating, getting down on my knees in prayer, or leaving comments on blog posts that imply my needs.

I have been praying for and trying to manifest the opportunity to meet more people in person, face-to-face, and to reach more people's lives by sharing my message of finding solutions instead of making excuses. All of that (plus filling out the application) was how I won the Amtrak Writers in Residency award and went off on an amazing trip to New York City, and it's essentially how I started this speaking and signing trip.

I have been doing podcast and radio show interviews since 2014. Every time I strap on my headset, I know it's an opportunity to make a new friend and build a relationship with someone who you can help or who can help you later on.

In January 2016, my interview with Super Joe Pardo was released on his show, the *Dreamers Podcast*. I had actually suggested he invite me to his other event, the Mid-Atlantic Podcast Conference, while doing the interview, but the timing just didn't work out, because he had already booked all the speakers.

As it turned out, if I would have gone, it would have meant that I couldn't go to New York during the Christmas holidays. I may have even talked myself out of accepting the Amtrak prize. So, when Joe asked me and a few of his other past guests about appearing at his first-time event called DreamCon, I knew I just had to accept!

Once Joe confirmed my appearance, I started sharing on social media that I was going to be at DreamCon, and inquired if anyone would be interested in hosting me.

As soon as one person agreed to, others started stepping forward with more opportunities. First was Al Chase, known as the Heart Warrior, who was also the Assistant Coach of the Buffalo Gladiators football team, who invited me to stay with him in his home. He is a real active member of his community, and I couldn't wait to find out what we would be doing.

Second was a lady named Ashley Coleman, from a site called the Blinkie Chicks, who contacted me after over a year of us not hearing from each other.

She said, "Max, is there any chance you could come to Raleigh?" She said if I did, she knew they could promote something at the Governor Morehead School for the Blind and at least one book signing, off-campus.

Third was Katie, the lady who was interested in buying the amusement park train, who said, "Sure, I'd love to meet you." Katie said she wouldn't let me ride her horses, but I could pet them and give them treats, and she'd do her best to describe the tricks they would do in return.

I knew I would have one week left before having to be back in Houston to follow up with my doctors, so I reached out to my Aunt Paula, who is more like a cousin because of her age and the zestful way she lives her life. She was one of the most positive people in my ears during the planning of my trip to New York City, and her Skype call while I was there was invaluable.

Aunt Paula said, "Sure, we can run around together." (That's a Southern term for "we will find something to fill the time.") She is also very active in the community, and I was sure she would come up with some great ideas of fun things for us to do.

Although the planned six weeks weren't jam-packed with activities and events, there were at least two important face-to-face meeting opportunities each week, and I was excited about the tour.

I love how it all started with my accepting one invitation and grew into something so much more. I love how people came forward to help—many of whom I never formerly asked to do so. I think they did that because I am so open and my desire to help others is genuinely apparent.

Before I finish this chapter, I want to comment on scheduling, in general. I'm a pretty free spirit. I choose to have faith and trust in both the Lord and in people that things will always work out. I like to believe that the events I'm meant to be at will become available, either through direct action or by way of friends, family, and fans deciding to reach out to me. I also didn't want a hectic, thrill-a-minute type of schedule. I love taking the train because it's a slower way of traveling. You can and will meet people and have leisurely conversations, as you will see in this book. You can also exchange emails and build friendships.

The best way to explain my approach to scheduling is to recount part of a conversation I had with Al Chase about spending time in Buffalo with him. He asked what kind of events I wanted to appear at, how many people I was shooting for, and how busy I wanted to be. I told him I didn't want to be one of those people who goes out on a book or speaking tour and comes back home so physically tired and mentally burned out that the first words out of my mouth would be "NEVER AGAIN!"

I wanted to have an easy pace that allowed for both work and fun. I wanted to visit some unusual places and experience some different types of foods. I wanted to talk to groups, based on whether or not my message would help them, not based on raw numbers or how much money they could spend.

I told him I wanted an equal amount of groups that might buy a book or hire me to speak as those that would include students, veterans, and the disabled.

I told him that I wanted to have new experiences to share on my blog, so that it didn't go quiet while I was traveling and then force me to work to bring my audience back to life once I was home.

The main point is that I think too many authors and speakers do what they think they should do, what they are expected to do, or what they see other public figures doing. I don't want to be that kind of person or the one to motivate others to do that.

I want people to enjoy their work. Otherwise, why not just get a job you hate to start with? It's much easier than making a living as an author, musician, filmmaker, speaker, video game developer, coach, or graphic novelist.

I also want to inspire and motivate people to do positive things with their lives.

Key Takeaways:

Plan on doing fun things during "work" trips!

Always ask others for what you want and need. Remember, "If you don't ask, they can't say yes."

Wonderful and unexpected opportunities will arise, if you reach out to your social networks.

Be open and make your desire to help others genuinely apparent.

Have faith and trust in both the Lord and in people that things will always work out.

Don't rush things; take the time to meet people, have leisurely conversations, exchange emails, and build friendships.

Don't do what others think you should do; do what YOU want!

Enjoy your work and plan on having new experiences.

Do positive things with your life!

Chapter 4: Having Faith and Investing in Myself

Once I decided I would go off to New Jersey and parts east, I still had to decide how much I wanted to invest in myself, because I wanted to bring along physical copies of my books to sell.

I had received some payments from my online publicity clients and had some extra money in my PayPal account that wasn't obligated to any specific bill. However, I still had the expenses of the trip as well as everything I had planned on my itinerary. I wondered if I could manage to do everything.

I did the math and ordered 40 copies of my first book to sell along the way, which temporarily emptied my piggy bank. My first book, *Leading You Out of the Darkness Into the Light* is the better seller of my first two books. I was both surprised and pleased when I discovered I ordered them just in time to slip them into my suitcase and messenger bag!

I didn't make any sales during the time leading up to the trip. I planned on ordering more copies of both, while on the road. I was hoping to have copies of my third book—

about my first Amtrak adventure—ready to go by the start of my trip, but the timing didn't work out, due to the availability of my editor and the fact that I delayed sending her my manuscript. In the end, I thought it was for the best, because I didn't want to put extra pressure on myself by being preoccupied with ordering, carrying, and promoting yet another book!

This trip would be about speaking, meeting people, and gaining exposure. I intended on learning lessons about doing book signings—including booking them, promoting them, and making the most out of them. Everything I learned would help me make the next trip all that more successful.

I encourage you to ask yourself, *What can I do to show faith in MY upcoming venture?* I'm not asking you to blow the rent money or live on ramen noodles. I mean, what can you do to show everyone, including yourself, that you believe in your project and know it will work out?

There is a line in the Bible about how God won't trust us with the big things until we prove we can handle the small ones. There is also the line about how faith without deeds is meaningless. I am still learning about taking action.

People think I'm fearless, but when it comes to money, I have a problem with investing it in myself. I struggle with spending money before I know where the replacement funds will come from. I have ruined or damaged relationships because I was too focused on the almighty dollar.

I'll never be a spendthrift. I've had too many years being the oldest brother and having the responsibility that goes along with that to spend quickly or extravagantly. A meager money mindset is an area that I work on changing all the time.

I have found that the more I trust in the future, the better that future turns out to be, and the more I invest in myself, the better things are. This is especially true when you outsource tasks to others.

More money started coming in after I started hiring people to do small projects for me. Quite often, it was exactly the job that I hired them for that made the money possible.

One great example is how I hired my friend, Michael Babcock, to set up FreshBooks for me. He created invoices and set up recurring billing cycles, which led to being able to collect money on a regular basis. Having that system in place came in handy when I needed money while traveling!

I will pray for the best for both of us. I can't wait to see how you decide to step out in faith and invest in yourself.

Key Takeaways:

Have faith in yourself.

Invest in yourself and hire others to help you.

The more you trust in the future, the better that future will be!

Chapter 5: Practicing My Signature

My family has never really liked the idea of my leaving home to go on adventures. However, no matter how much they hate my leaving, they usually come around and help me prepare for the trip. They make sure my clothes are clean and help me pack my suitcase. They make sure that I have toiletries and snacks for the trip. When they heard about my plans to sign books during this trip, they insisted that I needed to practice signing my name. So, I sat down at our kitchen table with some printer paper and a pen and began practicing.

I didn't have and still don't own a writing guide or signature guide for blind people. If you have never seen one of these, it is usually made of a plastic frame with wire strung across it, to simulate lined paper. (Now that I think of it, we probably could have made one ourselves. I bet my brother Michael could have whipped one up while I was staying with him, but by then, the signings were over, and I wasn't thinking about it.)

So, I took one of my books and turned it sideways. As I wrote a line of characters, I would move the book down so that I didn't write over what I had just written. I sat there for hours, writing the letters of the alphabet, in upper case and then lower case, over and over again. I sometimes got confused between the "p" and the "q."

By the time I left on the trip, my family said I had made a big improvement. But I could tell by the sound of their voices that maybe they weren't all that confident that people would want copies of my books after I had signed them! In truth, for most of my adult life, my signature has been horrible. One bank even made me sign a form saying that they should cash my checks even if the signature didn't match identically.

Michael told me I should just sign my initials instead of my name. I didn't want to do that, but I decided to use Max instead of Maxwell. No one ever complained about my signatures or the words I wrote in their books. In fact, most people were really impressed that my writing is as good as it is. However, it's possible that they were surprised a blind person could write, much less write legibly. I know my handwriting skills still need more work, and I intend to keep practicing. After all, that next book signing is always just around the corner.

Key Takeaways:

Your family and friends will likely and eventually accept whatever situation you decide to put yourself in, and offer to help you, regardless of their personal feelings.

Believe in yourself and your abilities, even if they are not perfect.

Chapter 6: Leaving Houston

My family and I went through the usual battles that precede any trip I take. I'm hoping that eventually they will have more faith in me and in the world at large to be less worried whenever I leave the house. Regardless of their worries, we rounded up my clothes and packed my suitcase that had the cow-print design on it.

On the day I was scheduled to leave (May 17, 2017), my cousin, Richard, drove me to the train station. I have never been comfortable with the Uber app. It always makes me feel like I'm one bad click away from ordering a luxury ride at peak times and getting a bill I can't pay. So, my cousin offered to check the Uber rates and drive me down for whatever they would have charged me. It turned out to be $40.

We had an uneventful ride. We talked about his genealogy research about the Wagner family—my mother's side of our family—and we talked about my trip. When we got to the Amtrak station, I got a surprise. My suitcase weighed in at over 50 pounds. Amtrak, like most travel carriers, has a limit of 50 pounds on checked bags. This is because they don't want their baggage handlers injured carrying your cases. I could have paid extra for a second bag, but that would have meant a $20 fee, which was an additional expense that I didn't really want. However, since I am all about finding solutions, I tried to quickly think of way to turn a negative situation into a positive one.

Then I thought, *Hey, I was a carnie. There has to be some stuff I can do without*. So, we first removed a pair of blue jeans. Even though I have lost a lot of weight, a pair of denim jeans isn't light. That wasn't enough, so I gave Richard my travel coffee mug, which took up space in my carry-on messenger bag. I wanted to make room for the toiletries bag that was originally packed in my suitcase. That did it, and they put my luggage on the train.

It would turn out to be the last time I would use my beloved cow suitcase. My family decided it was too worn out to keep using. It also had a couple of holes in it. I loved it because I could always describe it to people. When you tell people you are looking for the bag that looks like a cow, they never have trouble finding it. I remember posting a photo of me at the station with my bag and having another one of my cousins post that she wanted a suitcase just like mine. As usual, the Amtrak staff were great about taking me to the train before boarding, and they helped me find my seat. They then introduced me to my cabin attendant and went over my schedule with me again. I was excited about the adventure, but I was also dreading the layover in New Orleans.

It's a quirk of Amtrak that you cannot go from west to east or east to west across the Mississippi without having a long layover. I really wanted to change my route and go to Philadelphia by way of Chicago this time. The layover is shorter—only four hours in Chicago's Union Station versus staying overnight in New Orleans. Also, the waiting area in Chicago is much more comfortable than that in New Orleans. So, I sat back and tried to soak up as much comfort as possible in the reclining passenger seats. I was also not disappointed when the train made it into New Orleans late.

As I told the cabin attendant, "Every minute we were late would be one less minute on those plastic chairs or sprawled out on the linoleum floor."

I eventually ordered a cup of coffee and enjoyed the ride. It wouldn't be too long before my first new acquaintance would show up.

As I have written before, I love Amtrak—and trains, in general. I love how people are open to making new friends and having neat conversations, and how the slower pace of traveling by rail makes them willing to share about themselves and listen to your stories in return. So, I knew I would make some new friends.

It was just a matter of when and how many.

Key Takeaways:

Look at a bad situation and find a solution to turn it into a good one.

Remember previous times when you overcame challenging circumstances and use those memories to help you find solutions to your current problem.

Chapter 7: Walmart, Oysters, and Carla

My first new friend was made immediately upon boarding the train in Houston, Texas.

I met a lady named Carla from California. She was taking the train to Greenville, South Carolina, to visit. She was persuaded by her daughter to relocate to the west coast, but she still has many friends in Greenville. She is one of those over-the-top kind of people who says what she thinks and feels. The other riders called her "Walmart" because she had a huge amount of snacks and other supplies with her carried in a Walmart bag.

Because my budget was tight, I was watching my money. I was getting a bit hungry and trying to decide whether to eat another protein bar or buy dinner from Amtrak.

Carla asked if she could sit in the seat next to me. She was eating some oysters, so we began talking about them, in general. I prefer them fried. She likes them raw or smoked. She asked me if I wanted some, so I said yes. I wasn't sure what to expect, but I was happy to get them. It turned out that they came in a tin can similar to sardine tins.

She gave me some wet wipes and a fork. I really enjoyed them. I love trying new foods or trying new approaches to them. I took a forkful and was greatly surprised by just how good they were. I should also mention that unlike many blind people, I've never managed to figure out how to use a fork. I not only used the fork she gave me, but I also enjoyed it. I didn't have the usual fear I have when trying to use a fork in front of others. I thought I did a pretty good job. She noticed I spilled some of the oyster juice on me.

Carla said, "I don't want you to think I'm getting fresh, but you don't want this to get into your clothing," as she started dabbing up the spill on my pants. I just laughed and let her.

I was so satisfied with the canned oysters that I plan to buy more of them in the future, assuming there isn't some dietary reason why I shouldn't.

We talked about so many things. I was treated to a discussion about the proper way to prepare many soul-food dishes, such as pigs' feet, fried cabbage, hot water corn bread, and more.

I overheard her and other women talk about teaching their kids about raising their children. They talked about concerns with Social Security, SSI (Supplemental Security Income), and food stamps. Carla and several others in the car had ridden together from California and other places west of Houston, and had gotten to know each other. I was treated to lots of laughter, much of it on subjects or comments that were a bit racy. I loved how they didn't censor themselves. I am always honest and authentic, but I still sometimes choose my words more carefully than I need to.

I interacted with Carla again while waiting on the train to leave New Orleans, to head the rest of the east coast. Her friend, Cheryl, is an aspiring author who has been frustrated by multiple computer crashes and the inability to easily replace her last computer. People began offering advice. There was a real feeling of community in that particular train car.

Carla and I planned on exchanging email addresses before we got off the train, and we did.

Key Takeaways:

Random conversations can spark creativity, ignite laughter, and lead to new friendships.

New relationships can be found everywhere, if you are open to having them.

Chapter 8: Cliff

Let me tell you about Cliff. He was one of the passengers in the train car I was in. He is an older fellow from Montana. By the comments he made, I'm guessing his age to be in the 70s.

Cliff was going to New Orleans to visit his family. He said they would surely try, once again, to persuade him to move there, full-time. He said he was happy with the solitude. It's just him and his dog, up in Montana. They wouldn't let him bring the dog on the train—I'm guessing because Amtrak only allows small dogs or service dogs. I'm not sure.

I don't think Cliff is a doomsday prepper or a militia member. He seemed like a really good guy who just believes in self-sufficiency.

For example, he told us about installing solar panels on his roof so he doesn't have to pay for electricity. He mentioned having a back-up generator for cloudy days and a satellite dish for getting TV and the Internet. He even said that part of his summer plans included installing a solar-powered water heating system.

I was impressed that he can still be so independent at his age. We talked about my

47

first book, *Leading You Out of the Darkness Into the Light: A Blind Man's Inspirational Guide to Success*. He took a look at a copy and asked where to buy one. We exchanged emails, and I promised to send him a couple chapters of the book.

Those of us who were planning to spend the night in the terminal were rooting for the train to be late getting into New Orleans while Cliff was rooting for an early arrival and a Cajun dinner.

Key Takeaways:

Take every opportunity to promote yourself, your business, or your books, because you never know who might be interested!

Be sure to travel because you will meet interesting people.

Chapter 9: My First Book Sold on the Train

I met three people on Day One, then I was moved to the back of a car, and no one really came back there, other than the cabin attendant, a nice woman named Ashley.

I enjoyed talking to her, when she wasn't working. I told her about being an author and winning the Amtrak Writer's Residency. I had some copies of my first book with me and showed it to her.

She started flipping through it and asked where she could buy a copy. I told her: Amazon, my website, and from me. She asked if it would be okay to read a little of it and let me know. I said sure and told her my price.

When she came to the chapter about finding the positive in life, she said that was perfect because she has a partner who could use the encouragement and reminder that we have to *decide* to find the positive. Upon seeing that chapter, Ashley immediately bought my book, and everyone who overheard us talking were all interested and impressed. I have to remember to keep telling strangers I'm an author!

Now, if I could have done that a few more times between there and Philadelphia, I'd have been set.

I know it will happen. God wouldn't have allowed me to go on that trip if it wasn't meant to be, and that experience with the book sale is a reminder that even apparently confident people like me have areas where they need to get better at doing something.

I mean, I've never had trouble talking about my work. The problem comes in the lack of practice with a sale. I'm not yet smooth at it. Of course, this speaks to my authenticity. People don't want slick, superficial people; they want real, honest-to-goodness ones who struggle in their lives while simultaneously teaching them to improve theirs.

It was definitely an ego boost to have a stranger have that instant response to one of my chapters and want to buy the book!

Key Takeaways:

Remember to have confidence in yourself when you are promoting yourself, your business, or your books.

You will get better at asking for the sale, with practice.

If you are a creative entrepreneur, always carry copies of your books, CDs, DVDs, shirts, and any other merchandise you have with you, along with your business cards.

MAXWELL IVEY JR.

Chapter 10: Dave White, Inventor

During the layover, I was trying to get some sleep in the New Orleans terminal. Due to my budget restrictions, I was resigned to a long night of sitting in some hard plastic chairs, rather than enjoying the comfort of a hotel bed. Before I fell asleep or even got close to it, I met Dave White.

Dave and I chatted for a couple of hours. We are both really into our faith, and we talked about how God will always look after you. We talked about how you have to have faith in the small things in order to be trusted with the bigger things. I told him of my idea that we can't put limits on God.

Dave is a chef and an inventor. He was headed to Atlanta, to a new apartment and a new future of being in business for himself. He has patented a product called the Cake Cutter Carrier. (You can find him on YouTube.) It uses a cake-carrying box and with built-in blades to cut between 12 and 24 equally-sized, proportionally-shaped pieces of cake. He says it has applications in kitchens, bakeries, party shops, and even private homes. He told me he has a production agreement with a factory in China.

I told him about Tilman Fertitta's Billion-Dollar Buyer reality TV program and encouraged him to submit his product. We also talked about YouTube. He brought up his channel and played his video for me. I found out that he has been on YouTube for less than a year, has only recorded one video, and has over 500 subscribers. He really couldn't explain why he has so many followers on YouTube.

We exchanged emails. I entered his into my phone and sent him a test message to make sure I could write to him. He said, "Yes, I got it." So, I'm looking forward to following his progress and hearing about what happens with him.

Dave told me about his going through many life changes. Turning his experiences back to religion, he said that the Jews wouldn't listen, so most never entered the Promised Land. He said he felt like he could understand that type wandering in the desert and being lost for 40 years—between leaving the military and starting the design process for his cutter.

I don't know if I'm unique or just better at listening than most people, but I always seem to find amazing people who have great stories. That has not been just on the train.

I have connected with people in doctor's offices, at the carnival, and through online groups. I listen. Plus, like I have said before, you meet the people you expect to meet. I have a positive approach and am often blessed with having amazing people being put in my path. I love learning from them and also inspiring them by sharing my story.

Before I went to bed, Dave offered to buy me a bottle of water. I accepted. It really tasted good. Then, he told me he'd buy me a cup of coffee in the morning. He commented on how brave I was to get on the train and travel cross-country by myself.

Dave also helped me find a place to lie down. The floor wasn't much more comfortable than the chairs. I got cold, and I woke up with a sore back. It was better than having a sore butt! It's hard to believe that just 20 years ago, I could have slept in the back of a truck or on a ride platform and not been fazed by the experience. Actually, even though it is illegal now, one of my favorite places to ride was in the back of a pickup going down the highway. I could stretch out and feel the wind blowing past. Also, I have always been comfortable with silence. So, riding in the pickup bed gave me time to think. Of course, usually, my thinking would progress to daydreaming and then dozing off.

Key Takeaways:

God will put people in your path that you are destined to meet.

Have faith that things will work out.

Everyone has an amazing story. (Yes, everyone, including you!)

Chapter 11: The Topic of My First Two Talks

The problem with getting an opportunity like speaking at DreamCon is that you have to deliver on your promise. Up until the moment I got the email saying I would be included, giving public talks was a dream. However, it was something I could see myself doing, and it was something my friends—mainly my online ones—had encouraged me to try.

Suddenly, it was all too real. *What will I say?*

My DreamCon speech was titled "Just Press Send—Don't Let Your Fear Keep You from Your Destiny." My talk to the students at HopeWorks was about the same topic: facing your fears and overcoming them.

I could envision the general outline of my talks. After all, I know a lot about facing your fears, taking chances, stepping out in faith, and accomplishing your goals by taking one small step at a time. The real question for me was how to start. I also wondered how I would handle time management.

One of the reasons I put off doing my own podcast interview show was because of not knowing how I would end the recording at the proper time and still stay in the moment. I'm a big believer in getting in and staying in the moment. I have written about how my blindness allows me to tune out fear when traveling because I have to stay focused on all my surroundings to navigate my way around safely.

Those were some of the thoughts that were running through my head while I pondered the speech I was going to give.

I mention time management because I know I am horribly long-winded. I have difficulty giving short answers during interviews. I enjoy sharing my story and hardly ever wonder if I am sharing too much, but at DreamCon, I was only going to have 30 minutes to make my point about not letting perfectionism keep you from your dreams. My speech at HopeWorks was the second event that was actually scheduled for the day before the DreamCon event. There, I would have 45 minutes. The difference there was that my audience was younger, and I was told to keep my talk focused and to the point—or I will lose them. I hoped they would stay interested. I imagined they didn't get too many people like me at their events.

I often remind myself not to make assumptions. Expectations about you or your audience can lead to unnecessary mistakes. I reminded myself that while the event may be completely new to me in form, or the audience may be larger than I have addressed before, it's still the same thing—it's me telling my story, sharing my experiences, and making a point.

Although I still didn't know, exactly, what I was going to tell them, I knew that the hardest part would be the first few words out of my mouth. It was kind of like being on a roller coaster, where the scariest part is the long, slow ascent to the top of the first hill—or so I have been told, because I've never been on a roller coaster. But the comparison is accurate because they are both scary and until the day at DreamCon, I wouldn't have ever given a talk in front of over a hundred people before either.

In the past, when I performed at a church talent show, the hardest part was right at the beginning of my performance. As I thought about that experience, I realized that talent show was a great exercise and a timely reminder that I had the ability deep inside me to do this. I have the blood of performers in showmen running through my veins. Plus, being blind, not having to look into the faces of the audience helped me overcome the fear of speaking or singing in public.

Still, I think it's more about being in the moment. My friend, Amy Starr Allen, has heard interviews with opera stars in which they said that when you are focused on your heart's mission, you totally block out everything around you, including the fear.

I thought maybe the best place to start my talks was to admit my fears and tell people it is okay to have them. I thought I could start by telling the youth at HopeWorks, "I'm scared, all the way down to my toes." I could share that it was my first public talk and mention that I wasn't saying that for sympathy or to get a pass but to make sure they realize that I live my message every day.

To me, every scary event is an opportunity to grow as a person and to show others that the way I do it *works*.

As for the DreamCon folks, I thought of starting by telling them I wasn't ready to be there. I could go on and tell them, "But then, no one is really ever ready." I could tell them that the key is to admit you aren't ready, prepare like you are, and then do your best. After all, it's all about doing it better each time. No one is perfect—or even close to it— their first time out.

One of the problems is that too many experts give people the impression that they aren't scared or aren't the least concerned. The whole idea that you are expected to get to a point where the fear goes away altogether is also a lie.

I am not sure which John Wayne movie this comes from (it could be from *The High and the Mighty*), where a young pilot asks the Duke if he ever gets nervous. John Wayne's character says, "Son, if you ever pull that throttle back and don't get nervous, then it's time to turn in your wings".

A famous quote from John Wayne himself that relates to this is "Courage is being scared to death, but saddling up anyway."

The gremlins will always be there. Some of us are better at chasing them away. Others are better at making it look like they aren't bothered by the monsters of the mind. Most of us get scared every time we do it, no matter how often.

I know that has been the case with my writing. With my third book, I procrastinated for a month or more before sending it off to my editor. I didn't have anything better or more urgent to do. I just made up reasons and/or excuses not to press "send," because once you send the book to your editor, you are one step closer to sharing it with the world.

As I contemplated my dilemma, I decided to do what I always do when it's my turn to talk: tell the truth and be my authentic self. I will share a funny story and admit that I get scared, too. We all do… but we can face our fears and overcome them.

Key Takeaways:

Admit you aren't ready, prepare like you are, and then do your best.

You can overcome your fears by facing them, admitting you are scared, and by telling the truth.

Always be your authentic self.

Chapter 12: Arriving in Philadelphia

Joe Pardo, the DreamCon host, had planned to meet me at the train station, but there was a delay getting into Philadelphia. The Amtrak staff then made some type of mistake and I missed my stop, so they returned me to the station. (I'll write more about that later.) By the time I actually got to Philadelphia, Joe could not pick me up because he had another engagement. So, I took a taxi to the HopeWorks campus in Camden, New Jersey. It was an unexpected expense that surprisingly, did not cost that much.

Joe was able to meet me there once he was free. He then gave me a ride to my hotel. I checked into my room and went upstairs. I had a huge room with a couch and a king-sized bed. It was much nicer than any motel I ever stayed in while traveling with the carnival. (We routinely stayed in travel trailers, but we occasionally got a room, usually when working a short event.)

I had a great breakfast in the hotel diner. Afterward, I hung out in the lounge and waited until it was time to go speak to the youth at HopeWorks. I got to talking to one of the ladies at the reception desk. I explained that I was an author who was going to speak at the DreamCon event the next day. I left a copy of my book with her. I never got back to her to see if she liked the book or not, and obviously, I didn't get paid for it. But it felt good to hear the book had interested her.

After the talk I gave at HopeWorks, which I will talk about in the next chapter, Joe and I had dinner at a local restaurant. The food was good, and Joe and I had a good talk as I geared up for my speech at DreamCon the next day.

Key Takeaways:

Expect the unexpected!

Take time to appreciate your surroundings.

Chapter 13: Not Always a Confident Speaker

I received a couple of comments that concerned me.

One came in the form of an email from a lady who told me my exploits didn't inspire her. In fact, she said that hearing about everything I was doing made her feel like she wasn't doing anything with her life. I did my best to reassure her that I didn't come into the world this way. I told her about all the steps I took along the way, which allowed me to go from a morbidly-obese, failed carnival owner to a successful amusement-equipment broker to an award-winning author. I haven't heard from that lady again, so I hope she listened.

The other comment came after I gave my talk at DreamCon.

One of the other speakers, a lady with an amazing story of her own, said that I was inspiring. She said she actually agreed to appear at the event just to meet me. But she also said that I walked up to the microphone like it was just another day, just another step, just another experience. I was pleased that I gave off the appearance of being in complete control of the situation. However, I was surprised by the comment. I actually had some trouble accepting it.

I was a first-time public speaker in a room full of more polished and more experienced speakers. I just couldn't accept that I had done so well that people didn't know I was nervous. Or maybe I only said I was nervous because I was supposed to be anxious about talking in front of all those people.

I honestly don't remember feeling afraid when I walked to the microphone. I don't remember having butterflies in my stomach or sweating or anything. I think it is because I was focused on being in the moment. I was concentrating on putting one foot in front of the other and not tripping. I was running over my story in my head. I was hoping they would laugh when I got to the line about my first website being so bright that Stevie Wonder and Ray Charles could have had an argument about it. I was in the moment.

That a good lesson for you, for when you are afraid. Don't focus on your fear; focus on your mission. Think about what you are there to do and why. Then, just do it, one thing at a time. Slow yourself down and focus on what you are doing. Put everything other than your next task out of your mind.

Another thing that I realized only after my talk was over is that I had traveled over 1500 miles by train by myself. That only sunk in when one of the other speakers, Azuka Zuke, mentioned it from the mic. The distance I traveled wasn't something I thought about when preparing to go on the trip, or when leaving Houston, or even when giving my talk.

I actually didn't have a real problem with nerves until after the conference was over and I asked to sing in front of the DreamCon banner. I will tell you the full story about that in Chapter 14.

For now, I think it's important to share my speaking background with you.

In high school, I was not the outgoing person I am now. The last time I had to give a public presentation in class, I ended up in tears because the other people in our panel presentation stole all of my points before it was my turn. I had nothing left to say that was original and didn't want to just repeat what everyone else had said.

The year I graduated, I achieved the rank of Eagle Scout. I am one of the few blind people to do so. The ceremony where you receive your award is called a Court of Honor. Mine was a big deal. There were over a hundred guests and reporters from both newspapers who showed up. I was interviewed for TV, but all I could do when they called my name was stand there. I had no words. Thankfully, no one expected any.

In college, I got better. I ran for a couple of public offices and did much better sharing my thoughts out loud. However, I got a C in my class in public speaking.

I started thinking about the possible reasons behind my success in Philadelphia. I thought I had been preparing for being in public. I just didn't realize all the many ways this was happening. It's like that. Quite often, you can only see your path by looking back at the way you have come.

So, let's start with radio shows. I did my first one in February 2013. I appeared on the *Brian "The Hammer" Jackson Show* to talk about my amusement-equipment brokering site, the Midway Marketplace. (That was before I realized I could inspire others and became the Blind Blogger.) My first appearance was awful. First, my phone dropped the call. I was using a crappy Sprint flip-phone at that time. Then, when Brian tried to call me back, I accidentally hung up on him.

When we finally connected, he said, "What is your problem? Are you blind or something?"

I told him, "Well, yes, I am."

I know Brian wasn't expecting that. He went dead silent for over half a minute. Now, the last thing anyone wants in a live radio show is silence. Anything is better than nothing. Even someone cursing is better than silence.

Eventually, I laughed about the situation. Then, Brian started laughing, too. We had a great talk, even though it was short. He invited me on the following week. That show went much better.

I went on to do his show every Friday morning for about six months, then he and his producer had a falling out over a fundraiser they were working on. I didn't want to feel like the child of a divorce by taking sides, so I stopped doing the show.

(Update: since taking this trip, Brian and I have become friendly again. I've even been invited to come back on his show. That happened because I kept the lines of communication open. I found him on social media and shared his posts. I sent him the occasional email. In truth, I'm not one hundred percent proud of how I handled the situation, but I'm happy he is no longer mad at me, especially as those first radio appearances had a lot to do with my journey.)

Not having Brian's show to do anymore, I started reaching out to other hosts and I was invited by www.madlemmings.com's Ashley Faulkes to be the second guest on his podcast. We talked about building a new online business and the many challenges I had overcome to do that, as a blind person. Of course, Ashley reminded me the challenges were huge even for a sighted person. Next, I went on Alvaro Alvarito's *Low Vision Bureau* podcast. Then, I was off and running. I got a lot of practice telling my story.

I got used to answering many of the same questions over and over again. I got to the point I could almost anticipate when the host would laugh and for how long. I accumulated pet lines and shared favorite stories multiple times.

After I did more and more interviews, I eventually got invited to appear on online summits.

A couple, like the one hosted by Alex Okoroji, were done in a conversational style. Others, like the Virtual Success Summit hosted by Lolande V. Argent, were formal talks. I did very well at those.

Another thing that happened is people started asking me to sing during interviews. That started because my editor, Lorraine Reguly, encouraged me to put some personal stuff in my media kit. I mentioned that I love to sing. Hosts like to ask about personal items to make you appear real to their audience. They want you to connect.

One host asked me if I would sing something. I don't remember who it was, but

I said, "Sure, what the heck!" (I have now been asked to do this a couple of dozen times!)

I know a few professional performers. One told me that I was crazy to sing live and *a cappella* like that.

I told him, "Heck, you sing in front of several thousand people at your events."

He said, "Yes, but those are planned, rehearsed performances with musicians and all." That made me feel really proud.

I should also mention that I used to be afraid to sing in public.

When I was young, I loved to sing and sang all the time. In junior high school, as I was losing my vision, I mistakenly thought people who sang on TV did so without moving their lips. I tried to emulate them. People would make fun of me.

Then, my voice began to change as well. During a choir competition, one of the altos told me my voice sounded so bad I should just lip sync the words. Singing lost its joy then.

A few years ago, I wanted an intro for my first video. I didn't want to put off posting my first video because I didn't have a fancy intro, so I decided to sing a bit of "The Christmas Song" by Nat King Cole. People liked it.

I was encouraged. I continued singing in the intros of all my videos. I've even started recording full-length versions of some of my favorite songs.

I have days where I wonder if people like to hear me sing more than they like to hear me talk. The point is, I now have courage in my singing in public, be it on a radio interview or in person. So, the interviews and the singing had given me much more confidence about being in the spotlight. However, I still didn't know about being in public, as a speaker.

For over four years, I did everything online by phone, Skype, Blab, YouTube Live, etc. I ended up getting some good advice from a friend in church. Her name is Cassandra. She is a Jehovah's Witness, and yes, I am now one, too.

We met when she came to the door. We talked a while and started to become friends. She had been coming by the house to bring me CDs of music or of the Watchtower.

Just before my trip to New York City, she said, "Max, what would you think about coming to church with me? You know, it would be a good way to start getting used to being around crowds in anticipation of your trip to the Big Apple." I agree that it was a good idea. Our meeting halls generally only have about 150 people in them, but we can get very loud. We are a friendly, loving, and loud group. It turned out that being around more people more often was good preparation for my New York City trip.

I should also mention a little bit about how a Kingdom Hall meeting is run. (A Kingdom Hall is a place of worship used by Jehovah's Witnesses.) We start with a song and then a prayer. That is followed by a short talk on a subject to encourage us. It will lean heavily on the Bible.

We sing another song, then we have what is called the Watchtower study. That is where one of the congregation will lead us in a public study of a message from the national body. All the information is taken from or based directly on the Bible. During this session, people are encouraged to comment on what we are reading.

When you comment, you do that by speaking into a microphone so everyone can hear you clearly. They have members of the congregation walking up and down, bringing the microphones to the people who want to contribute. I don't know what urged me, but I started commenting, almost from my first meeting.

While my comments leaned more on personal experiences or my feelings about the topic being discussed than on scriptural references or Bible principles, my comments were welcomed. People came up to me after the meeting and told me how much they liked my comments. They encouraged me to keep sharing.

Hearing my voice over the public address equipment was unusual, but having a mic in my hand became much more familiar. Hearing my voice over the speakers didn't sound strange to me. It wasn't like hearing myself from a recording at all. You know how most people hate their voice when they hear it played back? In fact, I rarely listen to my previous podcast interviews or my past recorded messages because I don't like how I sound to my own ears either. But at the meetings, I could get an idea of how loud I should speak and how to control my voice. I just wanted to participate. I wanted to make my friend, Cassie, proud of me.

The other members told me how good my comments were and how much they appreciated me being there.

You know, I just had a thought. We have all heard of singers who recount how they began singing publicly in church. Well, someday, I may look back and think my career as a motivational speaker started in the Kingdom Hall in Conroe, Texas.

Later, I was invited to take part in Family Night (I won't call it a talent show because it wasn't a competition). The point is to invite potential or new members and their families to have a fun night together and get to know other Jehovah's Witnesses as regular people. There is food and entertainment.

I was invited to be part of a doo-wop performance of "Wonder Why" by Dion and the Belmonts. It was different being on a stage. When we stepped out there, the microphones had strangely disappeared.

I think I surprised myself and the other three singers when I took it upon myself to make an announcement. I told the audience that we were recreating doo-wop music from the 1950s—when guys would sit on street corners or front stoops and sing. They wouldn't have any instruments or microphones.

I said, "Not having a mic is right in style with our piece."

I would find out later that halfway through our song, a stage manager came out and put microphones in front of us. Being blind, I didn't see him. Being focused on the moment, I didn't hear him or feel the motion. It's a good thing that no one tried to tell me about them bringing us microphones while we were in the middle of our song! That is another example of where being blind can be an advantage. I wasn't disturbed by what was going on in front of us. I just kept singing. It was a great night. Everyone said we did great, and we got lots of applause.

I was much louder than the others, when I listened to it later, which may or may not have been due to the fact the microphone was placed directly in front of me.

Here is a picture of me with the three others I sang with. You can see the microphone that was placed in front of us. It's actually right in front of me and it looks like I am almost holding it but I'm actually holding my cane, which you can see, if you look close enough.

My last step prior to speaking at DreamCon, which I still consider to be my first public talk, was speaking to the students at HopeWorks, a non-profit group in Camden, New Jersey, devoted to training at risk young people for jobs in the computer industry and the Internet world. I was told I would have to be on my game because those kids are hard to keep focused on you.

I talked to them for about 35 minutes. I told a few of my stories. I answered questions. I was impressed with their lack of fear when it came to what they wanted to know, including one who wanted to know if I dreamed in color or black and white. (I mostly dream in black and white now, just so you know, although I sometimes have dreams that are so vivid that they are in color and I feel like they are real. I attribute that to having had perfect vision for several years before beginning to lose my sight.) I even connected with a couple of them on Facebook, after the event.

We had a great time. I was told the kids usually try to skip out as early as possible. I can understand that. (I was a good kid in school, but I wasn't above trying to get an extra day or even an extra hour away from class.)

The instructors left me alone with them. They said I must have done a great job because of all the laughter and loud voices. They also reminded me that not only did none of them leave when my time was over but also most stayed long afterwards.

I even autographed some of my books to those who wanted to buy a copy.

Here is a picture of me signing a book for someone after my talk at HopeWorks on May 19th, 2017:

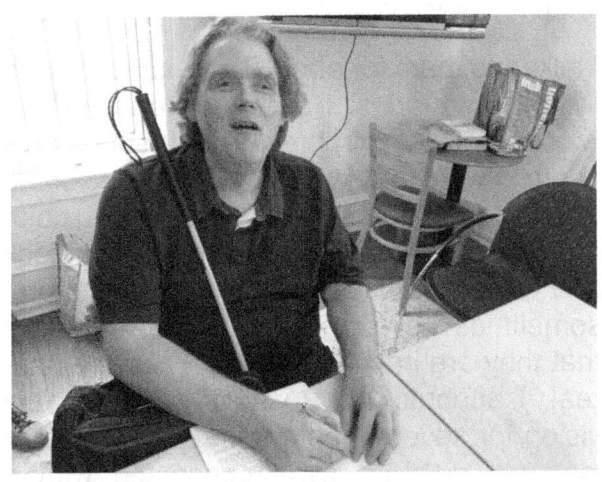

That picture is actually used on this book cover!

On Saturday morning (May 20th, 2017), I made my way down to the conference room where the DreamCon event was taking place.

That morning started with a wonderful surprise. A lady named Erica Blocker came up and introduced herself. She told me that the main reason she had decided to speak at DreamCon was so she could meet me. I didn't know her story at that time.

I would find out later just how amazingly strong a woman she is. I felt so much better after hearing that. I asked if I could give her a hug, and she said yes. I was the first speaker up after the introduction from the host, Joe Pardo.

Weirdly, that didn't even scare me, even though I wasn't originally scheduled to go first. One of the other speakers had a conflict or something and had to cancel.

I knew in advance that I would be going on first, but all I remember thinking is *Max, you've told these stories dozens of times.*

I reminded myself that no one knows my story better than I do. *Just tell your story and share the lessons.*

Something that occurred to me later is that people wanted to like me. People came there expecting to be inspired, and just by walking up to the front of the room and standing with the microphone in my hand, I had done that.

Often, all we have to do to inspire others is show up. It doesn't even matter if we do well or not. That is because so many others are afraid to show up.

Most will never force themselves to or give themselves permission to show up and be their true authentic selves. Most hide or hold back.

Here is a picture of me speaking at the DreamCon event:

That picture is actually used on this book cover, too.

Another thing I've learned is that even a bad appearance can have great results. My first radio interview was horrible, but it led to a follow-up interview and a regular guest spot.

At the end of my DreamCon talk, I gave myself a C+. I thought I rushed through my story. The audience—especially Joe—told me I was too hard on myself.

I spent the rest of the day hearing other more talented, more polished speakers with stories more powerful than mine tell me how inspirational I was. They told me how brave I was to come all that way by myself. They commented on how they were honored and proud to share the stage with me.

One of the speakers who mentioned me from the stage was Azuka Zuke. I'm mentioning him here because I was so taken by his energy that during the question and answer portion, I asked him to be my speaking mentor, and he said yes, which is another reminder of what I always tell people: "If you don't ask, they can't say yes."

Azuka will come up again later, which is another reason why I introduced him here. He is originally from Nigeria and made it to the United States with help from many people along the way. He now inspires and motivates people all over the world—through a series of best-selling, self-help books and by speaking at schools, colleges, and universities.

Azuka has a unique style that combines his powerful voice with an inspiring story and a series of selfie photos taken over the course of his journey. He often takes selfies with his audience during and after his talks.

I was never a great talker in high school or college. When I worked at carnivals, I used to be able to call people in on the midway, but I would have to work myself up to it. I would have to have a script of words I could say over and over without really having to think about it, such as saying, "It only takes one to win" or "You get a prize, every time." I also had to believe in what I was selling.

I really know, love, and believe in the package that is Max Ivey. Whether you call me Mr. Midway, The Blind Blogger, the Rock Star, Marvel's Daredevil of the Blogging World, the Blind Terminator, or the "No Excuses" guy, I'm here.

I've come a long way to get to this point, yet I have so much farther to go.

I want to give more talks and go out on a real honest-to-goodness book tour. I want to have my own coloring book or comic book. I want to record more videos and audios. I'd love to do an album of cover songs, and people keep telling me my life just screams "documentary film." Heck, maybe it's even a future blockbuster.

Since speaking at DreamCon, I have given talks and taken the stage at many places, including WordCamp (in New York City, in September 2018), MAPCON (Mid-Atlantic Podcasters Conference, in Philadelphia, in the fall of 2018), and the Podfest Multimedia Expo (in Orlando, in March 2019, and another in 2020). I gave a few talks to groups of visually impaired people, too, including an event at the Houston chapter of The Foundation Fighting Blindness (in May 2018), and another in southeast Texas (in January 2019). I will be sharing the stories and experiences surrounding these events in my next book, which will be the third book in my travel series (but my fifth book)!

I wrote this section to let you know that I didn't come out of the womb the person I am now. It's taken over 10 years to get here. I am 51 years old (at the time of this writing; I'm 54 now), and I finally feel I'm doing what I should be doing in the way I should be doing it. I finally feel like I'm close to being that person I was meant to become.

I hope you will remember this and start taking steps of your own. Find small ways to challenge yourself and improve yourself. Find fun ways to learn new skills and practice them. Like *Mary Poppins* says, it only takes a spoonful of sugar.

I didn't know all those steps were preparing me for standing on a stage or in front of an audience and inspiring them by sharing my life story, but here I am. I hope you will do the same.

I look forward to hearing some of the small ways you will develop yourself into that person you were meant to be. I love hearing about unusual solutions. I'm all about finding solutions instead of making excuses. So, put your thinking cap on and find ways to practice. The roller blade was developed so skaters could practice during warm weather months. The Kamikaze ride you see at fairs was originally called the loop-o-plane and was developed to train pilots during the war, and the telephone was originally intended to be a device to help the deaf.

Be open to those daily opportunities to grow. They are all around us.

I started doing radio shows because I didn't see a way to meet people face-to-face. I have a writer friend who used to think of her legal briefs as just another kind of storytelling. I can't wait to hear how you are going to apply these lessons in your own life.

Key Takeaways:

Everything prepares you for your future, in some way.

Take a small step every day.

Find small ways to challenge yourself and improve yourself.

Find fun ways to learn new skills and practice them.

Be open to daily opportunities to grow.

Don't focus on your fear; focus on the mission. Think about what you are there to do and why. Then, just do it, one thing at a time. Slow yourself down and put everything other than your next task out of your mind.

Chapter 14: Someone Bought Our Lunch

As one of the speakers at DreamCon, I was given a free ticket to the event, so I decided to invite my friend, Yvonne Garris.

Here is a picture of Yvonne and me at DreamCon:

Yvonne lives in Lancaster, Pennsylvania, within a reasonable driving distance from the conference center.

When making plans, I wasn't aware that the speakers would go out for lunch together, so I planned to go out to eat with Yvonne and her sister, Heidi. We drove for a while, trying to find a place that Yvonne had Googled earlier. We couldn't find it, so Heidi picked a place at random.

We sat at a table outside because the weather was nice. It also meant we were away from the crowds at the bar inside.

I had my first Philly cheese chicken, having already had my first cheesesteak the day before. I ordered it with sweet peppers. I had tried them the day before and loved them.

While we were sitting outside, eating our lunch and having a nice conversation, the waitress came out and told us that someone just tried to pay for our lunch.

Yvonne asked, "What do you mean?"

The waitress said, "Well, a gentleman put down $15 and told me to put that toward your meal."

I had this happen to me in New York City a couple of times. While there, someone at a neighboring table bought my breakfast, two blokes from England paid for a pedal taxi ride, and a cab driver tried to give me his umbrella. But this was the first time it had ever happened to Yvonne or Heidi.

It's quite a compliment when someone takes a liking to you to the point that they buy your meal. That experience is one of my favorite memories from that particular weekend in Philadelphia.

Key Takeaways:

Take advantage of nice weather.

Appreciate every experience because that's how memories are made.

MAXWELL IVEY JR.

Chapter 15: Singing at DreamCon

It's odd what affects us, emotionally.

You would have thought I would have been overcome by the trip to Philadelphia, the prospect of my first public talk, or how I was going to make the rest of the trip work out. I was actually hoping for one of those spiritually life-changing experiences that people talk about or that people like Elizabeth Gilbert (author of *Eat, Pray, Love*) write about.

The surprise was where the experience came from and why it affected me so completely—and this one experience rocked me all the way down to my toes. It even scared me a little, and you know I don't get scared easily. In fact, my friend, Cassie (Cassandra, from church), told me that she wants me to call her the next time I think I might get scared because she would like to see what that looks like.

What I'm talking about has to do with an event that happened after the conference was over. It still puzzles and even unnerves me.

At the end of the day, everyone was taking photos. There were group shots and selfies.

I decided to ask them if I could sing before they put all the cameras away.

They all said sure, and Joe arranged the recording. In fact, in the video, you can hear us sorting that out prior to me singing. I sang "The River" by Garth Brooks. It's kind of my theme song. I usually sing it or "Angels Among Us," by Alabama, in such moments.

So, I stepped in front of the event banner. I was standing next to Travis Wolfe, preparing to sing, when it happened.

I don't know if it was nerves. I just know my whole body was taken over. My legs were wobbly, my stomach felt tight, my heart was beating rapidly, and I had that weird feeling in my throat you get when you are sick.

I don't know if you can see it in the video, but Travis tried to help hold me up.

I had to actually concentrate on my breathing and think of the next word in the song and what notes to sing.

It must have had an impact on the other speakers because Azuka Zuke told me that I should sing every time I give a talk. He is known as the selfie speaker. He takes selfies with his audience members before, after, and sometimes during his talks.

He said, "Max, you could become known as the singing speaker."

Even though I trusted and believed Azuka, I didn't put his advice about singing when speaking into practice right away. I had to work up to it.

The first few times I sang at subsequent speaking events, I credited Azuka and told the audience I was singing to make him happy, as if I had to explain why I was going to sing.

The more I did it, the less I felt I had to justify or explain why I was singing.

The feelings I had during those moments didn't go away. In fact, whenever I talk about it or write about it, those feelings come back. A week later, I still wasn't sure what they were. Part of me hoped the feelings would go away, and part of me wondered if I would ever be blessed to feel them again.

I know it's the failing of us as human beings to try to figure everything out.

Travis said, "Max, just thank God and be grateful."

Eventually, I would do just that. But for a day or more, I tried to figure it out. The reason is that the feelings made no sense.

You see, I've sung that same song dozens of times. I've sung it on live radio shows with audiences of thousands of people—of 10,000 to 50,000, and even more. I never got nervous. If that is what nerves are, I was never affected in that same way.

I shouldn't have been nervous. I was singing in front of the other speakers—a room full of authors, coaches, and podcasters—many of whom have even more powerful and inspiring stories than mine.

If there is anywhere I should have felt at home, it should have been at that very moment.

Maybe because I could see them as my people—my family in life, so to speak—had something to do with it. Maybe only in the company of such a group could I allow myself to feel those emotions.

After all, it was great people such as them (and my wonderful friend, Adrienne Smith) who convinced me of my value as a role model who could inspire others.

That is why it is so important to build a community of friends who will tell you the truth about yourself.

We rarely see how special we are through our own eyes.

Here is a picture of me with some of the other speakers at DreamCon, standing in the same spot where I sang (from left to right is John Casto, me, Travis Wolfe, Erica Blocker, Aimee Joshua, Azuka Zuke, and Joe Pardo):

As I write this, those same feelings are coming back to me, and I am starting to believe that is the message.

I wrote in my book, *Leading You Out of the Darkness into the Light*, that past successes helped me overcome the failure of my family's carnival business and with the transition to being an amusement equipment broker and later an author, coach, and now, speaker.

Well, now I have that one special moment. As I continue to progress along the path toward whoever it is I am meant to be, I can always go back to that moment at DreamCon. I can close my eyes and go back there. I can think, *I did something really scary, and it all worked out.*

I call that controlling the movie screen of your mind. We all do it. We replay past experiences in our mind's eye, but most of the time, people replay only the negative moments of their life. They recall the tragedies, setbacks, and failures instead of the successes, or they recall the successes and criticize themselves for not having made more progress since those happy occasions.

We have to not only play the good memories on that jukebox of the mind, but we also have to use them in a positive way. Decide to use those past positive experiences to motivate you to do more today, instead of asking, "Why haven't you come, Father, since then?" If you already have a goal, then take action toward achieving it. If you aren't sure about what you want to do next with your life, then take some time and use a systematic approach to deciding what your goals are. That will require researching potential goals and how you would go about achieving them. It will take soul-searching to decide what it is that would make you truly happy. It will take creativity to find ways to make that goal a reality, given your current circumstances. You may have to ask for help or find a mentor, and you will certainly have to change the way you see yourself.

I've gone from a guy who only knew one thing—the carnival business—to someone who saw other possibilities as he learned how to create an online business, then to realizing that my work can *and does* inspire others.

I used to say, "I'm just a guy who shows up and works his butt off to build a business to help support his family. I'm nothing special."

I could have let my blindness be an excuse. I could have chosen to let my disability be a reason not to try. I finally realized that because I didn't do that is why people are inspired by my story. However, it has taken time to come to that realization.

Remember that you will change, as you are moving toward your goal. You will learn and grow. You will probably find even more challenging goals to aspire to, once you get started.

The singing shouldn't have been scary. It should have felt safe. But I thank God I was affected.

Even now, I feel my heart racing and my eyes tearing up, as I write this.

Key Takeaways:

Remember to play back your successes in the movie screen of your mind.

If you already have a goal, then take action toward achieving it.

If you don't have any goals, create some.

Change the way you see yourself, if need be.

Build genuine friendships with others and believe them when they tell you truths about yourself.

You will be surprised when something profoundly affects you.

Chapter 16: Azuka Rescued My Books

After the photos and videos were taken, I had to get on the road quickly.

I was short of money, as I had often been when traveling.

I had already checked out of the motel and moved my suitcase into the trunk of Heidi's car. Actually, I had borrowed money from Joe to stay another night in the hotel, but then my friend, Yvonne Garris, invited me to stay with her, so she helped me check right back out again. Before losing her vision, she used to work at a hotel, so she knew I would not have any trouble getting that money back since I hadn't actually used the room that day. Yvonne specializes in helping the newly disabled. She also works with people on finding or regaining their confidence.

I was in such a hurry that I completely forgot about the copies of my book that I had left out on a sales table. To show you how unprepared I was, that first time out, there wasn't even a price tag or sign with the books. There also wasn't anything to tell the hotel staff who they belonged to. When I realized I had left them, my original thought was, *Oh well, they will end up in a trash can or something,* even though I hoped that someone would see the book cover and decide to read them or share them with a friend, family member, or co-worker who could use some encouragement. I've read about how top self-help authors like Wayne Dyer used to give away books or cassettes to people who they thought needed to hear their message and then had great stories to tell about how someone contacted them to tell them how much that gesture had changed their lives. So my next thought was, *Hey, maybe that could be me.* However, I wasn't really expecting that to happen.

After I arrived at Yvonne's house, I got a call from Azuka. He told me again how inspired he was by my talk and my courage to travel so far all by myself. We talked about my speaking and how I might further my career. He then told me that he had picked up those books and taken them home with him.

I said, "Great! I was worried they might have ended up in the trash."

I also said that as long as someone got some good out of them, I wasn't worried about the cost.

Azuka surprised me when he said, "Max, I'm going to put them out at my speaking events and try to sell them for you." He went on to say that he would send me the money when they were all sold. I had a good feeling about Azuka, so I put it out of my mind.

Later that winter, I got a check from Azuka. When you get a check, you cash it. He messaged me about it. He said that he wasn't able to sell the books, but that he wanted to invest in me and my mission. I didn't even think about refusing. I have learned about the foolishness of pride and/or false modesty. If he wanted to spend his hard-earned money on me, then I was honored that he thought enough of me to do so.

But that isn't the end of the story.

Azuka decided to give those books away, but he didn't just give them to anyone. He donated them to libraries in Africa.

Now, Azuka is too modest to have told me that himself. I know that because an amazing young man contacted me through Facebook to tell me how inspiring I was. He had read my book, *Leading You Out of the Darkness into the Light,* from what amounts to his high school library. Talk about being blown away. I know those kids have it rougher than most high school kids in America, and I'm sure he has had it harder than I did in school. But he found me and my story inspiring. I told him I hope to someday be able to visit his country and find out what happened to him and to any others who were affected by reading my books or Azuka's books—or both. It's the kind of event that makes you want to write more often.

Azuka and I have become great friends, and I can't wait until the next time I get to meet him or share the mic with him—maybe in Atlantic City, for the Mid-Atlantic Podcasters Conference, or MAPCON.

Azuka is a master at booking himself to speak at high schools and colleges, as well as at fundraising events. So, I imagine that if I ask, he will be able to make it happen.

I can't tell you how much I'm looking forward to seeing him again. He has had a big impact on my speaking career. After all, he gave me the courage to start singing as part of my public talks, and I can always count on him for words of encouragement on those rare occasions when I get just a little discouraged about the progress of bookings.

As a speaker, going from giving volunteer talks at conferences or for local groups to paid speaking events is a very difficult jump to make. Getting the bookings or exposure that will lead to those paid stages is hard to come by. Like how a lot of people often feel, there are times when my progress isn't coming fast enough to suit me. When that happens, Azuka is one of my close friends who I know will encourage me to keep doing what I'm doing.

I know he will tell me, "Max, it's just around the corner."

Because of Azuka, I now post on social media that I'm available for speaking. I mention how I will share my hilarious journey from failed carnie to successful equipment broker, etc., and I continue to send out pitch emails.

While I'm still seeking a career as a paid speaker, I've realized that "paid" doesn't always have to mean a check. It could be the opportunity to sell books, merchandise, and consulting services from the stage. It can be a group purchasing copies of my books in advance to cover the costs of visiting their city. It can also be a person or company covering my expenses instead of writing me a check.

To that end, I now tell people that if they want to book me and they don't have the ability to pay in cash, they can cover my traveling and living expenses. Thanks to trial and error, that list is now more complete. I tell people they need to provide a plane or train ticket, Uber costs, baggage fees, a safe place to stay, wholesome food, good coffee, and transportation in and around their community while I'm there.

I truly love sharing my story and inspiring others to start writing about or sharing their own. I love meeting people face-to-face, making friends with them, and helping them to grow. I enjoy having time to explore the local area and have real local food with great people. Although I would love to be getting paid several thousand dollars every time I take the mic, what's important is getting my needs met, having the opportunity to bring in some income, and getting the chance to challenge others to overcome their excuses.

Whether you want to hire me outright or book me to speak in exchange for my expenses, you can learn more about what I will talk about and watch videos of past talks on my website, The Blind Blogger, on my speaking page.

Key Takeaways:

Opportunities lie in the strangest places or circumstances.

People will invest in you and your message.

You need to advertise or mention your products and/or services on social media.

Surprises will come to you and you will inspire others.

Money is not always what is important.

Chapter 17: Money Problems

Yes, I started the trip with a very tight budget.

What money I had actually came from the Midway Marketplace—what I think of as "my day job." I had sold a park train, back in December 2016. The buyer wanted to show his appreciation for me and my site as well as the role we played in getting him and the previous owner together. I later found out that he had somehow ended up with two trains. He wanted to keep the better of the two and find a new buyer for the Casey Jones train. He asked me to help with that, and he gave me an advance against my commission to cover the cost of creating the listing on my site, which actually led to a new policy where I now require all equipment sellers to put up an ad listing fee.

That advance gave me the money to purchase my train ticket to Philadelphia and to pay for my hotel there. I was still hopeful that Joe would be able to provide some or all of my lodging. Come to think of it, I never asked him about him or one of his friends hosting me while I was in town. Of course, DreamCon was held at a hotel, and he got a special rate for the conference presenters. Given that, we would all congregate at the hotel. That made a lot of sense. However, it was a case where I didn't even ask. I should have.

I actually paid for my room one night at a time. I was thinking that something would happen, and it did. It wasn't what I planned, and I made things much harder on myself, thanks to my pride where it comes to money.

Here is the full story of what happened.

I asked Joe to loan me the money for the room.

At lunch, I went to eat with Yvonne Garris, a friend from up the road in Lancaster, Pennsylvania, and her sister, Heidi, instead of going to lunch with Joe and the other speakers. I mentioned that already. What I didn't tell you is that during the lunch, I asked Yvonne and Heidi if I could come stay with them for a couple of days while I solved my money problems.

Yvonne said, "Sure," so I went home with her and her sister, Heidi. She even told me to ask the hotel about getting my money back for that last day.

I packed up my suitcase and moved out of my room right after lunch.

I got back to the conference a little late, but I didn't miss too much. At the end of the day, I repaid Joe. I didn't have to do that right that minute, but I felt like I needed to. Part of that was because I was raised to pay people you owe, but more of it was pride in not having to borrow from the event organizer. I would have hated for the other speakers to find out the inspirational man who came over 1,600 miles by train by himself was broke.

I went home with Yvonne and I enjoyed a great couple of days there. I got to try red beet eggs and have some great talks with her. (Red beet eggs are boiled eggs soaked in red beet juice and sugar. They are very tasty.) While at Yvonne's, I also got to spend time with her dog and cat. I've always enjoyed the company of pets and am always happy when I get to stay with someone who has a friendly fur baby for me to enjoy, too.

Another thing I did while there was to record an episode of my podcast, *The What's Your Excuse? Show*. My guest was Carol Pepino, who is known as "Carol the Connector." She and her husband were traveling around the country in a recreational vehicle, teaching people to take control of their medical treatment. Her husband had a stroke and was only saved by her intervening in his care. Following that interview, she invited me to come on a tour with her, but after over 20 years of dragging myself around the country in old trucks and travel trailers, the idea just didn't appeal to me. It wasn't until long afterward that I realized I made an assumption, which I never challenged until working with Lorraine on editing this book. I should have asked about where I would stay and what the conditions would be like. Maybe they were going to be traveling in comfort and style! That realization is a good reminder of the dangers of making assumptions. Next time, I will definitely ask questions before giving an answer!

Back to my money problems.

Because of returning Joe's loan, I didn't have the funds to pay for the train to Buffalo, where I was going to stay with Al Chase.

I started asking quietly for help. I reached out to people who had talked about buying a copy of my book. I followed up with people who might hire me for getting them booked on podcasts and radio shows. Finally, I called my host, Al, and asked him for a small loan. He said sure and gave me his credit card information over the phone so I could purchase the ticket.

When Al met me at the station, I can't tell you how happy I was. I had a big smile of relief on my face as we drove to his house with the windows down, a beautiful breeze wafting through his vehicle, and classic rock tunes cranked up on the radio.

I stayed with Al and his girlfriend, Deb. They fed me, took me places, and bought me meals, etc. (I'll elaborate more on what else we did, later.)

Here is a picture of me with Al:

Al took me to a restaurant called Jim's Steak Out, which in the Elmwood Village neighborhood of Buffalo. I had their signature "Stinger," which is a steak and chicken finger hoagie. It was delicious!

Here is a picture of me eating it:

Just after the first of the month (in June 2017), I received some money, so I went to the bank and withdrew it. I repaid the loan for the train ticket and gave Al some money to help with the costs of hosting me. I didn't have to do that. He hadn't asked for any money or even hinted at it but I had the voice of my dad in my ear telling me you really should give him something for his troubles.

Doing that left me short again. I finally paid for my next train ticket with a combination of credits from Amtrak and a new online media client.

I had decided a while back that the best way to reach authors was to reach out to publishers, editors, proofreaders, cover art creators, and all the other service providers required by self-published authors. I had connected with Wade Fransson of Something or Other Publishing (SOOP), LLC. He had agreed to hire me to work on behalf of his author clients.

I reached out to him and said, "Hey, I'll give you a better rate if you will pay in advance."

"Your rates are perfectly fine now," Wade responded. "I want to see you succeed because you can offer a service our authors need, which we are not ready to provide, and you can do it at a reasonable cost. So, why not just invoice me for a retainer to be charged off as you get my clients booked on radio shows and podcasts?"

Wade did, however, add that he wanted to be first on my list of people to find the bookings for, because he is also an author. He was in the process of publishing his second book, a continuation of his memoir, which shares a larger-than-life sort of personal history.

He sent me the money just in time to board a train to head to Jacksonville, Florida, to spend some time with my brother, Michael, and his family.

I should have reached out to Wade sooner. It was only after being honest about my situation and asking for help that my immediate money problems were solved.

At that point, I still wasn't sure where the money would come from to get me onto South Carolina and then home to Houston. I had a ride sale pending, but some purchasers are horribly unreliable. Even when sales happen, they never happen on time.

However, I had faith that I would be taken care of, somehow.

I didn't want to ask my family. I also didn't want to openly ask for money on social media. I didn't want to feed the fears of my friends and family or have them think I wasn't safe. I don't mind people finding out I'm not as financially successful as I'd like to be. I just didn't want too many people worrying for no real reason. Many of them have fears for me already and don't need a real-life example of why I should stay home, where it's safe.

But I have to share this story, because the one thing I really believe hurts more people than just about anything else is the people out there who make their lives seem amazing because they only share the positives in their lives. The setbacks and our solutions are the best parts of the story! And I would never rob someone else of the power of a great story and how it may influence them to take risks and take action to go after that big goal in their lives.

Key Takeaways:

Setbacks are opportunities to find solutions.

There is danger in making assumptions, so make sure to ask questions before providing a response.

Honesty and authenticity are important.

Stories influence us to take risks and actions to pursue our dreams.

Chapter 18: Book Signing at Dog Ears Bookstore & Café

Al picked me up at the train station, and considering how much trouble there had been coming up with the money, I shouldn't have been surprised that the train was late. Neither of us had signed up for the app to give you updates on arrivals, so Al was basically hanging out, waiting for me.

I talked to him twice by phone but the reception was poor. Trains travel through a lot of wide open spaces where cell service can be spotty, at best.

The train was late because Amtrak was doing maintenance on some of the rails, and priority is given to trains hauling freight over those carrying passengers. A couple of men got very frustrated and attempted to leave the train. They were informed by the conductor that if they left the train, they would be on private property and subject to arrest for trespassing. They calmed down, and eventually, the train got rolling again.

People ask me why I don't get upset in situations like that. My response has to do with the pragmatism that comes from a long life.

First, when a train breaks down, you almost always still have air conditioning or heating, working electricity for charging your devices, working bathrooms, access to cold drinks, and possibly even Wi-Fi. While a delay means you might miss a connecting train or make a friend or loved one wait for you, it's far more comfortable than I remember from traveling with my family's carnival, when one of our trucks broke down.

In the days before cell phones, breaking down might mean spending the night on the side of the road with no food, nothing to drink, and having to use the bushes as a restroom. I have also learned that there are very few plans that can't be rearranged, and sometimes, those delays lead to meeting a great new friend. Other times, being late means you missed being part of a wreck. I also think the fact that my dad was never really ever in a hurry plays a part in this attitude. Heck, he spent half of my life telling me to slow down and not walk so fast!

Before we went to Al's house, Al took me to visit a local wrestling academy. One of his friends teaches people how to do the moves and prepare to wrestle for a living. I didn't feel up to taking part, but I enjoyed sitting there and listening to them work. I was surprised that the instructor spent so much time on how a move sounded as well as what it looked like. As a lifelong fan of pro wrestling, it was cool to get a little bit of the behind the scenes of the profession.

Al was a great host, as was his girlfriend, Deb. They treated me to great food—both local favorites and some of Deb's Italian family's recipes. My favorite was her Buffalo chicken dip. Al and I started most days with cereal and good coffee. Thankfully, Al had good coffee. We ate twice at a local pizza place where Al sometimes helped out.

Al also took me to a meeting for a local non-profit. I got to meet the young men they were trying to help, and I got to hear a talk from ladies representing a national non-profit, who were there to inspire the kids. We had some pretty good spaghetti as part of the evening.

I was supposed to speak to that group while I was in Buffalo, but I guess you could say I got bumped. I hope to get to address the group, should I ever visit Buffalo again.

Al introduced me to his friend, Andre Robinson. Andre hosts a live video podcast on Facebook Live called *Rise Up Sports National*. Because of Al, Andre invited me to come on the show. It was unusual for several reasons, which is what made it so much fun. It was me and three other guys hanging out talking about sports—no self-help, no inspirational anything. I felt like I held my own, except for not knowing that my own team, the Houston Texans, weren't doing as well as I thought they were. In fact, our top wide receiver was one of the worst in the league at that time, although my impression was he was doing much better.

I had a great time with the guys—before, during, and after the show. I was added to the show's family and given a shirt and a hat to wear.

Eventually, it would be time for my book signing, the main reason I was in Buffalo to start with. Yes, I was there to meet my friends, Al and Deb, and enjoy the city, but between us, the event at Dog Ears was the main event of my stay there.

I had my first ever book signing at Dog Ears Bookstore & Café on June 2, 2017. Despite all the work done on social media by me and the store's owner, Thomas (Tom) McDonnell—including a newspaper article— the event was not a success. No one came, and obviously, I didn't sell a single book. We were beaten out by uncommonly beautiful weather in Buffalo. People chose to spend time out in the sun instead of coming to a book signing.

I was told by the owner and by Deb that they get so few great days like we had that day that people love to be outdoors. She said that if we had been on a patio, we might have had a chance. But in May, people are starting to recover from the winter months that come with rain and snow—sometimes feet of snow—and being stuck inside for days on end.

Here is a picture of me at the book-signing table:

I always try to look for the positives instead of focusing on the negatives, in almost every situation, and try to find lessons from every experience. There were several positive things about that experience, and I learned a few things, too.

First of all, I had a great conversation with the store owner, Tom, and one of his employees. They are both authors, and we talked about the age-old choice between being traditionally published or self-publishing.

Second, Tom provided my guide, Deb—Al's girlfriend, who took me to the book signing—and me with some excellent warmed pita bread and hummus.

Third, when I got home, I found two wonderful emails in my inbox. One was from a gentleman who has been following my blog and told me I was inspiring. He said he wanted to talk to me about doing more in his life. So, I may have a new client for my coaching services.

The second email was from Pipe and Thimble, who operate a bookstore in California for only indie authors. They are also publishers. Their goal is to give the authors they select the services of a publishing company without the author relinquishing the rights to their work. They said they were interested in hosting me for a book signing and have also suggested the possibility of my doing a "No Excuses, Take Action" workshop. With much more lead time, I believe they will do a much better job of getting the word out about my visit to their store. They also offered to help me with contacting fellow store owners to arrange events prior to and after spending time with them. Unfortunately, nothing ended up happening with them because they either closed down, went out of business, or moved on.

What did I learn? I realized I missed a few opportunities. I should have offered to sign a copy for the store owner. I should have offered to leave copies of my books with him on consignment. I should have interviewed him for my podcast or for a future blog post.

Tom and I ended up talking months after my visit there. He even requested that I send him some copies of my books to sell in the store.

As for action taken to distract me from my setback and keep moving toward my ultimate goal, I recorded some videos, after being reminded how powerful my voice can be. A friend had heard me sing part of "One Good Well" by Don Williams. She said it would help her if I sent her the audio file to listen to. She was grieving over having to cut off life support to a family member.

I was shocked to find out that my simple version of a favorite song could comfort someone going through something so tragic. It got me off my butt and got me moving.

I've talked about offering a talk called "Music and Motivation." It's something I've thought about for a while but done nothing. Instead, what I did was write a couple of blog posts and then uploaded my files to YouTube, first as private videos that I could share with friends to get feedback. I made the videos public, afterward. Then, I recorded and uploaded Part Two of a segment on asking for help, something I'm great at and that I believe in.

I will continue singing and recording my thoughts. I love to sing. People enjoy my singing, and sharing my voice may help open their hearts and minds to my words.

The next part of my trip involves spending some time with my cousins in Aiken, South Carolina. Even though I wasn't sure if I would have a book signing or a speaking engagement while I'm there, I was positive that I would do something exciting and fun, because I am really good at seeing life as an adventure.

By the way, I have since had more book signings after publishing my third book, including one at a place called the Book Scene, in Houston, Texas, on March 24, 2018, and another at Half Price Books, in Austin, Texas, on June 3rd, 2018.

The stories surrounding both of those adventures (complete with pictures, which includes a press release Lorraine wrote that my local newspaper printed, word-for-word!) will also be mentioned in my next book—along with all of the speaking events I mentioned earlier—which will be the third book in my travel series (and my fifth book)!

Key Takeaways:

Look for the positives instead of focusing on the negatives, and try to find lessons from every experience.

Remember that life is an adventure!

Chapter 19: Foot Problems

I hate to bring this up, but I need to mention that while traveling, I had a recurrence of the issue with the sore on my foot.

Prior to going to New York City, I had gotten a cut on the bottom of my left foot. Not being able to see it and having a lack of sensitivity in my feet, it went untreated. Eventually, I had to go to the emergency room for intravenous antibiotics and then underwent a long series of treatment from a podiatrist.

While at Al and Deb's place, my foot started bleeding again. I thought that might happen, so I had packed Epsom salts in my bag in case I had to soak my foot.

After soaking it for several days in a row at their house, a thick scab finally broke lose. However, that meant my foot would bleed for most of the trip—usually only slightly, but I had to pay attention to it.

I didn't want to injure my foot further or allow it to get infected, so I had to get them to help me put antibiotic cream and bandages on it.

I'm mentioning it now for two reasons. The first is to remind you that your physical, mental, emotional, and spiritual health are critical to success in business or in chasing your dreams. The other reason is that this is going to come up again later in the trip.

I'm so happy that the people I stayed with were so forgiving about the problems caused by my foot. I'm sure Deb had to clean up blood from her house after I left.

Key Takeaways:

Your physical, mental, emotional, and spiritual health are critical to success in business or in chasing your dreams, so make sure you don't neglect yourself in any of these areas!

Don't hesitate to seek help from someone, whether you need it or not!

Chapter 20: Visiting Niagara Falls

Near the end of my stay with Al and Deb in Buffalo, Deb said that I couldn't end a visit there without heading up to Niagara Falls.

I had been wanting to go but didn't want to come out and ask them to take me because I understood that it would be a pretty long drive. I also figured that like most tourist attractions, it would be expensive. So, I was very happy when they volunteered.

(In case you don't know about Niagara Falls, it's a group of three waterfalls along the border of Canada and the United States.)

As we got out of the car and started walking, I noticed something I should have expected. It was all downhill, which meant that when we are through enjoying the sights—or in my case, the sounds—we would have to walk all that way back up again.

Before having gastric surgery and changing my lifestyle, I would have never made it. Back then, I would have to take breaks just to walk from the parking garage to my gastric surgeon's office, but I put it out of my mind. I knew I wasn't that same person anymore, and I sure as heck wasn't going to pass on an experience out of fear of a hard walk.

We walked around, and I got to feel the sheer power of the waterfalls. I mean, they have an energy that is truly rare in nature, and even without seeing them, I could appreciate their magnificence. Also, there was a mist in the air from all that water crashing down nearby. We got a late start, so we didn't have time to take the boat ride out into the water above the falls. We also skipped the walk through the caves. And since I didn't have a passport, we couldn't go across to the Canadian side.

While there, I had a great moment over a small thing. Al decided we should get ice cream cones. In the past, I might have declined, worrying about getting it all over me—or asked if they had a bowl or a cup I could get mine in. I'm a messy eater, and ice cream is tricky under the best of circumstances. Plus, this would be ice cream outdoors. But I thought, *What the hell*?

So, I said, "Sure."

When Al asked me what flavor I wanted, I didn't play it safe and try to think of what flavor might be the easiest to eat. Nope, I went for peanut butter chip.

When we sat down to eat them, I got another surprise. They weren't small cones, stingily filled. They were very large cones, and it seemed like the shop owner had piled the ice cream up to twice the height of the cone. But

I didn't rush. I enjoyed my ice cream. I had to use half of a bottle of water and some napkins to get my face clean, but it was worth it.

I know it doesn't seem like much, but it's all about deciding. In this case, it was choosing what I wanted instead of saying no or playing it safe. I didn't even think about ordering mine in a bowl, which is my usual go-to with ice cream.

It was then time to go home, but my day of taking risks wasn't over.

On the way down to the falls, I noticed there were people playing musical instruments and singing. So, I asked Al and Deb if they would record me singing.

Yes, I sang "The River" again.

In the video, my voice is drowned out in some parts by the water from the falls, but it felt so great to do it. It had never entered my mind to wonder if I needed a permit or permission. In fact, no one even noticed what I was doing.

The video got thousands of views on Facebook, which was really cool, and now I can say I sang "The River" at Niagara Falls.

Here is a picture of me standing by the waterfalls, where you can see the mist in the air:

Considering it was only a few hours out of the day, it was an amazing experience. It was a reminder of just how amazing God's creations are. It was also a reminder of just how small we are—a very humbling experience—and it was very tiring. I can't honestly tell you about anything else that happened that day or night.

I'm so thankful to Al and Deb for their friendship, for allowing me stay with them in their home, and for giving me that day.

Here is a picture of me with Al, and one of me with his girlfriend, Deb, by the waterfalls:

The next time I'm in the area, I'm going to do it right. I'm going to visit both sides of

Niagara Falls, ride the zip lines, take the boats, walk the caves, and sing by the waterfalls again.

As we were leaving, I heard that the bar there has a nightly karaoke contest where people compete to see who can sing "The River" the best. You had to be there at midnight to collect your prize. Next time, I'm going to compete, and I bet I win. And as long as I'm sharing dreams, next time, I plan to record my own music video.

Key Takeaways:

Take time to enjoy and appreciate the magnificence of nature.

Don't let anything stop you from going on an adventure.

Take some risks, instead of playing it safe all the time.

Dream, and dream big.

Chapter 21: Changing Plans After a Talk Fell Through

As you know, much of my first speaking and signing tour was dependent on help from other people.

While I did my best to book my own events or to book events in addition to those promised by my hosts, for the most part, I was unsuccessful doing so. Sometimes my hosts were unsuccessful, too. So, the question you are probably asking is "What happens when a booking falls through?" Well, in my case, it really depends on the booking. I'm going to share what happened when my talk at the Governor Morehead School for the Blind fell through.

It seems that the lady who invited me had not given enough thought to how my being there might affect the students taking their final exams. It may also have been that my scheduling wasn't as well thought out or as clear far enough in advance.

I was planning on staying with my host, Ashley Coleman, or at the school itself. I was actually looking forward to staying in a dorm-style room and interacting with the students all week. I was hoping to make some new friends and get inspired myself by their stories. When my talk fell through, it also meant my lodging fell through. I would have been fine with the idea of paying for a hotel or motel, if I could have found other events. However, I was unable to find a library, bookstore, or non-profit group willing to have me give a talk during that week.

I thought, *Well, why not visit some family?* My cousin, Rocky Ivey, had offered to have me stay with him when visiting. I got in touch and asked him about that. He ordinarily would have loved the idea, but he and his family were moving into a new home. I then contacted a few friends in Atlanta about doing something there.

My one friend, Deb Krier, was headed to Kansas for a family event and was very disappointed she couldn't help me. My other friend, Anna Banguilan, reached out to a lot of people but had no success, given the short notice.

So, I thought, *Why not go see my brother, Michael?* I had not seen him for four or five years. He was in Houston for a couple of days when our youngest brother, Patrick, had a heart attack, but he spent all of his time at the hospital with my mom while I spent most of the time at the house with my nephew, Seth. Well, someone had to watch Seth, or maybe they thought someone should look after me. Either way, Michael and I didn't get to spend any quality time together during that short visit.

I reached out to Michael but didn't have any luck getting a hold of him right away. I then reached out to his ex-wife, Michele. At that time, they weren't a couple again, but they were friendly and Michael was spending a lot of his time at her house. Until I heard from Michael and Michele, I was kind of stuck. Finally, Michele responded through Facebook that, yes, I was welcome and to come on down there. So, I went ahead and booked my train ticket to Florida.

While I was happy to be headed to Michael's, it would mean not getting to visit Katie, the lady who ended up being the new owner of the park train. I was disappointed because I was really looking forward to getting to learn more about her Lipizzaner stallions, but I was really happy to be headed anywhere.

I always knew I would figure something out because that's who I am and what I do. Thanks to emails from my blogging mama, Adrienne Smith, and my friend, Lorraine Reguly, I've learned to accept that about myself. Lorraine likes to say that I get into more shit than anyone else she knows, but I always manage to come out of it smelling like a rose, finding the positive in every situation, thus having a great story to tell! Over the years, I've learned how to just find a way. It's partly because I decide there has to be a way, and I keep looking for that solution, no matter how crazy it may seem at the time, and once I find a solution, I take advantage of it, even if it makes me look silly. A dirty, grimy, smelly solution is better than no answer at all. Plus, with over fifteen years in the carnival business, I learned about finding a way to get to next week. As podcast host David Ralph once said, "My days in the carnival world were like a PhD-level course in hustle and muscle."

I hope you will start following my example and decide there has to be a way to continue moving toward your big goal or dream, and act on whatever solutions you find.

I was told that Michael would be working until the weekend, so I'd be staying with Michele until then. Before I got to Florida, I found out that Michael had changed his schedule so he could pick me up at the station. It turned out that the ride from the terminal in Jacksonville to his place was over half an hour. The station was roughly halfway between his house and Michele's, and neither was what you would call close by.

That is one of the downsides of traveling by train. Often, you can't get to the exact town you want to get to. Sadly, our government is considering closing or shortening the hours of even more stations.

Michael took me home and we hung out at his house. He is a real tech guy, and I had fun with him when he showed me his gadgets, including Amazon Fire and Echo, which I fell in love with and want in my house now. He loaded up the house with food. He still had to go to work driving a truck, so I stayed with his little dog, Eva. We spent time together as I watched TV shows.

The last time I saw Eva was when my dog, Penny, was still alive. Eva didn't like Penny. Well, that's kind of an understatement. Eva continuously tried to attack Penny! That was very annoying but a little funny, too. I mean, a dog weighing less than ten pounds barking and growling and leaping at a dog who weighed over ninety pounds! Penny was such a laid-back dog that she just let Eva do her thing. Eva just didn't want another dog in her house. I understand.

Sadly, I had to think that maybe our family hadn't been together for a while because our dogs couldn't get along. I know it was the distance and the fact that my younger brother, Patrick, and Michael both had busy work schedules that got in the way. I hoped that it wouldn't be the last time I visited my brother and the rest of the Houston Iveys again.

I enjoyed getting to binge-watch *Lewis* while petting Eva. I couldn't get that show on Netflix and I don't have an Amazon account. After my experiences at Michael's, I thought about getting one. Maybe I will even get to the point where I'm one of those people who carries his Amazon device with him and learns to plug it into whatever TV he has access to, wherever he is staying. I'm going to talk more about Michael's house later.

Right now, I want to talk about having to adjust to multiple new houses and homes while traveling. A lot of people have asked me how a blind guy does that. I have also heard from sighted people who have commented on the difficulties and stresses of sleeping in different beds while traveling. I know it's a lot different than my carnie days when I lived in a travel trailer, where the worst part of the week was getting to the next lot and waiting to find out if or when I would have access to water, sewer, and electricity. Some weeks, you would be at the new location for a day or two before you had the usual comforts of home.

My experiences during my carnival days actually helped me adjust to various new surroundings. For example, when I was growing up, we lived in one trailer where my bed was a wooden platform with a mattress over it. During one stretch, we lived in a trailer where I slept on the floor. That trailer would leak when it rained and I'd have to twist my body around until I found a space where I didn't get wet. So, sleeping on a plain mattress on the floor like I did at Al's house or having a twin bed like I did at Aunt Paula's house or sleeping on a pull-out couch at Yvonne's house wasn't that big of an adjustment to me. I think it's much harder for people who are used to really comfortable beds in their homes. Also, those who travel more obviously will adjust better to the changes. They will also appreciate their homes more when they get back to them.

With the exception of the hotel I stayed at in Philadelphia, Michael had the most comfortable bed. It was a king-sized bed that originally belonged to my grandmother, Mary Wagner, and had made the rounds among various family members. At one time, it was even my bed when I was living and working in Oklahoma. That was when I had taken a real job for the Internal Revenue Service (IRS) and before returning to join the family business.

Making adjustments also applies to bathrooms. Being a big guy, at six-foot-four and a bit over 260 pounds, bathrooms are a bit harder. Nothing is worse than having to bend down to try to wash the soap or shampoo off of you, and I hate it when the water just trickles out. At my home, we are blessed to have a shower with plenty of hot water and very good water pressure for those luxuriously long hot showers I love.

As for laundry, I was blessed that people I stayed with offered to do that for me. I could have done my own, but it's difficult because no two washers or dryers are alike. And unless a machine is brand new, it will have some quirks to it. I'm not allowed to do the laundry at home because I once melted a mattress cover by drying it on too high a heat. Even though I replaced it at my own expense, the decision was made.

"Max, you don't need to do the laundry anymore."

Now, the independent part of me knows I should be able to help out and do my own laundry, but the honest side of me thinks that if all it took to get out of doing laundry was to ruin a mattress cover, I would have done that years ago!

Just like finding your way around a new neighborhood or city when you move to a new house, you venture farther and farther, the longer you are there. I usually have to be somewhere for a few days before I start trying to make my own coffee or prepare my own food. Mind you, my abilities there extend to making a sandwich, pouring a bowl of cereal, and putting something in the microwave. Those are so easy that even this blind guy can do them!

Actually, my hosts often apologized for offering me simple, home-cooked foods. It's like they expect me to be disappointed in good, old-fashioned family food. But my lack of skill in the kitchen and my general approach that everything is to be savored means I appreciate any meal I didn't have to prepare.

I'm also happy that no one ever asked me to help with the dishes. I would have, if asked, because I am, in fact, very handy when it comes to drying dishes. It's something most people could probably do with their eyes shut!

Key Takeaways:

Be prepared to change your plans, if need be.

Adjusting to something new can take time.

Be grateful for your blessings and the things you take for granted.

Chapter 22: Meeting Craig in New York City

Once I was sure I was welcome at Michael and Michele's houses, I bought the train ticket and looked at the route I would be traveling.

As it turned out, to get from Buffalo, New York, to Jacksonville, Florida, you have to go through New York City and spend the night in Penn Station. Now, if I had some extra money, it would have been fun. I could have found out if NYC really is the city that never sleeps or not. Unlike New Orleans, Penn Station is open 24 hours. But with no money to spare, I spent the night stretched out on a bench. It was a big improvement over the chairs or floor in New Orleans.

I slept most of the night using my messenger bag as a pillow. Thankfully, I can sleep just about anywhere. That train station was a challenge, with the constant announcements of arrivals, departures, and reminders about the dangers of unattended bags, but I managed several hours of sleep there.

In the morning, one of the staff helped me to find the bathroom and the Starbucks, and then, I boarded the train, to continue on to Florida.

On my way from New York's Penn Station to Jacksonville, I rode across the aisle from a fellow named Craig.

He was doing something I would have never thought of—and I think we've established that there is very little I wouldn't consider. Skydiving, white-water rafting, and bungee jumping are off my list, but I'll try a lot of other things, and we have already talked about my willingness to adopt unusual solutions to difficult problems.

Craig was moving to Florida and he was using Amtrak to move his belongings. He told me that with Amtrak, you get two carry-on bags and two checked bags that can each weigh up to 50 pounds. I only brought one checked bag, when leaving Houston, but it could have been a case of misunderstanding the rules due to the pressure of getting myself situated well in advance of the train leaving the station. I knew about the weight limit because my suitcase was two pounds over it when I boarded the train in Houston.

What I didn't know is that for an extra 20 bucks, Amtrak will give you four more boxes or bags—not just one! So, Craig had loaded up his stuff and was moving to Florida. After we started talking, I also found that we had both worked for the Internal Revenue Service. I had answered phones in an automated collection center while he had been a revenue officer. More often than not, he would have been the guy we called if an account was over a certain dollar amount or involved employment taxes. We talked about the stress of working for the IRS. He told me that the accounting work wasn't very stressful; it was the caseloads that finally got the better of him. He said the longer you are there and the more cases you work, the more they give you. He didn't say it, but I wondered if he thought maybe it would have been better to have been a slacker in the beginning. These are the kinds of odd thoughts that sometimes come into my mind.

Craig talked about having had some troubles with drugs and later with gambling. He was headed to Florida to live with his parents. At least, that was where he was headed temporarily. I asked him what kind of work he was planning on doing. He said his health wouldn't allow him to do accounting anymore. He was talking about doing affiliate sales marketing. I told him of a friend of mine who had made his first big sale as an affiliate marketer. I agreed there can be good money made at it.

I happened to overhear him tell his mom that he only had five bucks on him. I knew from previous experience that it would not buy him much to eat, so I gave him a couple of dollars in change.

Later, he asked if I had a card. I didn't, so I gave him a copy of my first book. After a while, he said he liked what he was reading and that I could expect to hear that he was working the exercises.

I don't mention this to brag. I mention it because it's proof that I still have a rescuer's complex when it comes to money. I have to try hard not to be affected by hard luck stories, even when they aren't being purposely told to pull at my heartstrings. I've been hungry before—not so much since I quit traveling with the carnival, but it's happened. I just have a hard time knowing someone else is going through that feeling. Even though I didn't have much money, I still helped the guy out because I wanted to.

Craig helped me with refilling my water bottle and finding the restroom, and he and one other passenger followed me off the train to make sure someone was there to meet me and get me home.

My brother, Michael, told the one fellow that he didn't know how I did it. I am assuming he meant traveling by myself and depending on others—mostly people I've never met before. I usually meet good people, but then, I don't usually hang out in parking lots or alleys. We are talking Amtrak. They have a lot of attentive, friendly staff who look after me, and I get a discount for being disabled. I don't mind taking the discount. Usually, it covers the taxes, but more importantly, it means that my ticket shows I may need assistance. Every time someone scans that ticket, they will be reminded to look after me—and let's not forget traveling by myself is part of my story. It started with Amtrak when I won their Writer's Residency award and decided to go to New York City for the Christmas and New Year's holidays. I ended up going by myself because I didn't have anyone who could go with me, and it's become part of my overall inspirational story.

I enjoy taking the train. I enjoy the conversations I have and getting to know people from all over the country. I look forward to someday taking trains all over the world.

Key Takeaways:

Meeting new people can be fascinating and talking to people helps you appreciate them more.

Help others whenever you can, if you have the means to do so—and even if you don't.

Chapter 23: Michael's House

Now, I will tell you about Michael's house and my time with him. Then, I'll tell you about my time at Michele's house and what happened there. The reason for the split narrative won't surprise anyone.

My brother, Michael, and Michele were divorced and living separately when I visited Lake City, Florida, where they live. Michael works a lot, driving a truck for Purina and selling on eBay. During the week, he and his faithful dog, Eva, live at his home, a mobile home. On the weekends, he heads over to Michele's and spends his time there with her, his kids, and grandkids.

Michael and Michele are vastly different people and live in much different homes. Michael's is a mobile home, and it's not in the greatest shape. That is mainly because a couple of years ago, some squatters moved into his home and took it over. They did a lot of damage that he just hasn't had the time to get fixed yet. His porch is tricky. The steps twist up to it. I'm not sure if that was done by the squatters or is just the product of a mobile home in the Florida climate. Still, he had to guide me up, almost carrying me, at one point. Once inside, I didn't complain about the fact that we didn't go very many places while I stayed with him. I actually dreaded going up and down those steps.

During the week, I worked on my laptop and watched TV, but true to my word of finding enjoyable experiences everywhere, I loved it. That is because Michael had Amazon Fire on his TV. I had been dying to try one out in person but didn't want to spend the money and then find out it wouldn't work for me. Since you can never know if new technology will be truly accessible by a blind user, I'm often a late adopter. For example, I didn't replace my old flip phone with an iPhone until 2014.

Michael had to manually activate the accessibility features so it would talk to me. Once he did that, I had a lot of fun exploring the menus and finding out what movies and TV shows I could watch with it.

There was so much available content that Michael came up with a game. One of us would pick a year, and the other would pick a number. Then, we would watch whatever movie came up. I got lucky both times we played.

We watched *The Wizard of Oz* and *American Graffiti*. He also reintroduced me to *Dr. Who*. I was disappointed that none of their offerings came with described audio, a feature that uses an off-screen voice to narrate the action for blind viewers.

I'm a big fan of British TV shows, especially their crime dramas. I love *Midsomer Murders*, *Prime Suspect, DCI Banks*, *Inspector Lewis*, and *Inspector Morse*, but many of those shows are not available through our cable package at home. I went crazy binge-watching *Inspector Lewis* and *Dr. Who*, to the point that I maxed out the data on Michael's satellite plan.

I guess I should mention that where Michael lives, he doesn't have cable, so he depends on a satellite Internet connection through Verizon. They put limits on how much data he can use. Not usually being at home much, that was rarely a problem for him. With me there all day, I almost ran up his bill. Thankfully, he noticed it in time.

He said, "Max, just don't fall asleep watching it again."

I decided to try out the mobile hot spot on my cell phone. It worked great, meaning that at least my laptop Internet use wasn't counting against his limits.

Due to concerns about space in my suitcase, I left my CPAP machine at home. I use one of those machines to treat my sleep apnea, which isn't as bad as it was prior to losing over half my body weight following the gastric surgery I had. I can go without my CPAP for short periods of time. However, the longer I go, the more likely I am to fall asleep while reading, watching TV, or doing other sedentary activities, so I was careful to listen to Michael's warning about falling asleep while watching TV.

(On a future trip, Transcend™ provided me with a small portable machine, so that I wouldn't have to choose between quality sleep and my suitcase being overweight.)

Michael stocked up his refrigerator with things I could microwave and showed me how to use his machine. He bought coffee I could make in there, too. Michael doesn't usually drink coffee. He's a Pepsi or Diet Pepsi kind of guy. He often brought lunch and dinner home. There is a great Chinese restaurant near where he lives.

Some other things about his house include the fact that there is a problem with part of his roof. While waiting to get time to fix it properly, he rigged up a device to drain water from the roof into his kitchen sink. It meant that anytime I would go in and out of his kitchen, I would have to duck, so as to not knock his contraption down. I got a little bit of a kick out of it. It was like being a carnie again and just making due.

His tub and shower worked just fine, and he gave me the better of the two beds.

Something else Michael did was give me his old iPad.

Michael has always been a tech guy. He always has the latest gear. For example, he's the only person I know who bought the first iPhone when it came out in 2007, even though he had to switch to AT&T to get it. He had previously ordered the latest model of the iPad Pro. It came while I was there. I actually had to hold his dog, Eva, while the FedEx woman brought his new toy. I failed and Eva got loose, but the driver had no problem corralling his vicious Chihuahua.

After Michael got his brand new one, he asked me if I wanted to take his old one. An iPad was something else I had been thinking about getting, which would mean a costly investment that came with a usage concern. *What if I get it and then can't use it?* Even though I have an iPhone, that thought still ran through my mind. But it was free, so why not?

"Hell, yeah!" I exclaimed.

I had trouble at first. Even with my large hands, it felt huge when I tried navigating the screen and figuring out where things were on it. But I accepted it, and Michael helped me get it switched over to my Apple iTunes accounts with all my own passwords on it. Like anything new, it was very slow going at first. As I installed apps on it, like Netflix,

SiriusXM, and others, I started enjoying it more. When Michael gave me his older Bluetooth keyboard, things got even easier. I could actually see myself not only using it but also embracing it and enjoying it. I could see it becoming indispensable. In fact, by the time I went on my next trip, I hoped to be able to do everything I do with my laptop from my iPad.

I may even get a newer one, because I realized that having to carry a heavy laptop plus its charging cable in a messenger bag around my neck is just not good for my personal well-being. Swapping my laptop for an iPad would drop pounds from my shoulder bag and take a lot of strain off of my neck and shoulders. It might even help lessen the numbness in my hands. I was actually scheduled to have more tests to isolate that numbness, so I agreed to be back in Houston by June 27th. That was actually the reason why my first speaking and signing trip wasn't longer.

I was grateful that Michael helped me solve the problems around my fear of buying an iPad. He advised me that iPads get stolen more often than laptops, so I will have to be more security-conscious when traveling with it. Michael also advised me to leave it in my bag where people wouldn't be able to see it and listen to it through headphones while using my miniature keyboard. Funny, he was more concerned about someone stealing the tablet than he was about someone trying to take my wallet. However, I rarely have a thousand dollars in my wallet.

I should mention that Michael has always helped me. In fact, it was because of him that I got my first Mac laptop. I was the victim of several Windows computer crashes in a row. At that time, Michael had heard that Apple had started including a screen reader called *Voiceover* on all their desktops and laptops. He finally talked me into getting my first Mac by buying one on eBay and sending it to me. That was one of the best gifts he ever gave me. It also made me a lifetime fan of Apple products. Now that I think about it, a lot of my story might not have happened without him. Besides the tech help gave me, he filed for my domain name for the Midway Marketplace, helped me build my first website, and he sent me some of my early carnival ride-listing clients.

One other thing I did at Michael's house was drink beer. I had sodas and coffee, but he also had beer. I don't know what brand it was. He told me it was weeks old, but it was cold and tasted good enough to me, so I drank several of them. I actually drank one or two just about every day. I never had a taste for beer, wine, or mixed drinks before. Of course, people don't usually encourage guys my size to drink, worrying about the possibility of having to fight me or help carry me home. Plus, my dad was very anti-alcohol, anti-tobacco, and anti-drugs. He had seen too many people from his youth end up being ruined by alcohol and drugs. Luckily for me, I never smoked. I've also never dipped snuff or chewed tobacco. They just never interested me. So, I watched TV, ate good food, drank Michael's beer, kept his dog company, and played with my new tech gear.

I should mention one thing about his dog, Eva. It's been years since Patrick, Seth, my mom, and I have visited Michael in Florida. I hate to admit that, but I think part of it was the fact our dogs just didn't like each other. Penny was 90 pounds and one of the coolest, could-care-less dogs God ever created.

Eva is a little Chihuahua who runs her house. When I was there, she was a perfect host. She let me pet her whenever I wanted and whenever she felt like it. But when she and Penny were under the same roof, that little dog wanted to fight Penny every five minutes. I guess it's just what happens when some other dog comes into your house. I know it's a long drive to Florida and back, and Michael and Patrick both work hard, but I'm sad to say our dogs probably had quite a bit to do with keeping us from seeing each other more often.

When Michael wasn't working and was home, he and I had some good talks. We talked about technology, the carnival business, my websites, my trip, and much more. We watched TV together and just hung out like a couple of guys. We ate food from take-out containers, so there were no dishes to be done.

When I asked Michael what people in Lake City do for fun, he said, "Well, there isn't much here." He said most people who come to Lake City are on their way to places like Disneyland and Lego Land, where there are things that are more fun.

I think Michael is a lot like me. I don't think he needs a lot to be entertained. Of course, he has his family on the weekends, but during the week, I think he can always find work or play to keep him happy. He spends a lot of time in his truck, delivering cattle feed, and he has a lot of equipment in his house for printing the merchandise he sells on eBay. I can't tell you how many printers he had but I had to work around them when walking around his house.

Next, I'll share some of my experiences with his ex-wife, Michele.

I will tell you this much: Michael and Michele are about as alike in their homes and housekeeping as Oscar Madison and Felix Unger from the famous TV show called *The*

Odd Couple, but when they are together, it's obvious that they care for each other—and they unite to be amazing parents and grandparents.

Key Takeaways:

Remember to take time to enjoy the little things in life, like eating, talking, and spending time with your loved ones.

Create a game to play while doing simple activities such as watching TV or movies, to intensify the fun.

Don't be afraid of trying new things, including new methods of technology, because they might end up being more beneficial to you than may realize!

Chapter 24: Annoying Quirks

On the way from Michael's house to Michele's, I realized that I have a quirk that is very annoying. I'm sure I have more than one, but the one I'm speaking about now has to do with water bottles.

In our house, we don't recycle anything. They don't offer recycling in the town we live in. So, to cut down on the number of bags of garbage we have to carry out, we crush and roll up the plastic water bottles before throwing them in the trash can. I've been doing it so long that I don't even think about. I also don't notice just how much noise is created by rolling up a water bottle, and I must confess to having some pride in just how tightly I can compact a water bottle. I think I may even be competitive. Like I said, I've been doing it so long, I didn't even realize it was a habit.

I drank a bottle of water in the truck, on the way to Michele's. When I got there, I rolled up the bottle, making a big racket. I woke up one of the grandkids and Michele. She was very gracious and treated me well. Michael was more bothered by it than she was. I felt a bit self-conscious about it. I thought, *Oh, hell, I haven't seen her in years, and now I'm going to start off by making a bunch of noise and waking up sleeping kids.* Those are the kinds of things I think about. They are probably the kinds you think about, too. We are always playing the scenes in our minds, usually with worse outcomes than those in reality, and it got me thinking about what other things I do that are annoying that I do out of habit.

One I thought of is when making coffee, I will fill the water well of our K-Cup® machine right up to the top. That is because I have trouble pouring things. I usually use an oversized mug to make it more likely that the cream and sweetener will end up in the cup. By filling the machine up to the top, it often spits water out of the bottom. As a result, I often get water on the counter. I do my best to clean up after myself, but I don't always get all the water wiped up.

Also, the bottom of the machine sometimes collects water and will grow mold. So, I'm working to try to remember to only fill it up to the actual line. I'm also trying harder not to use more cream or sweetener than I really need. And I now check the catch plate under the coffee machine to see if it needs to be cleaned because letting mold accumulate can be very dangerous to the health of everyone in the house, not just the ones who drink coffee. I'm also realizing that I'm more rigid than I thought. For example, when told

I was getting water from the shower on the bathroom floor at home, my response was "the shower curtain isn't high enough." When my mom bought a waterproof rug to put down, I balked over having to set it out before showering and pull it up when I was through. My family relented, and we agreed the rug could stay down all the time.

They also bought a new shower curtain.

The problem was caused by the facts that I am so tall and I enjoy standing under the shower, feeling the hot water beating down on my neck and shoulders. Because of my height, some of the water was actually bouncing into the rest of the bathroom.

Another thing is that I can't sleep well, until I take my socks off and fold them up, something that has always gotten me in trouble with my brothers. I fold them because it's the best way to make sure you don't lose socks. Most blind people have clips they use to keep pairs of socks together in the washer and dryer, but I don't, so I fold them. I don't think it is really an annoying quirk because my mom was always complaining to my brothers, asking why they couldn't also roll up their socks.

When I sleep, I have to pull the covers up so they are over my shoulders. No matter how warm it is, I can't sleep until I'm covered up. A sheet will sometimes do, but usually, you will find me with a blanket covering everything but my head—with the air conditioner on high. Also, I can't sleep in a room that is too silent. Over the years, I've fallen asleep to the noise of generators or people out on the midway. I've stayed in travel trailers where having a TV or radio on was often necessary to drown out the noise from the neighboring trailers. The particular quirk of being unable to sleep in a really quiet room got me yelled at by my host, Mark, in New York City, during my first trip there. Several times, he had to remind me to turn my music or TV shows down. I don't think I really understood just how much sound travels in an apartment. He would send me text messages asking me to turn it down before his neighbors complained. I actually thought he might give me a lower rating with Airbnb because of it, but he didn't, giving me five stars as a tenant.

Yet another quirk about me is that I don't enjoy traveling anywhere if I have to ride on the left side of the vehicle. This applies to planes, trains, cars, or buses.

I'm used to being in the front seat, on the passenger side, and leaning my body toward the passenger door. I'm so used to that side that I actually have trouble getting in and out of vehicles from the driver's side, such as when riding in a sedan or the back seat of a four-door pick-up. I sleep better leaning against the right-hand door as well, and since I can't appreciate the scenery rolling by, being comfortable for a nap is high on my list of travel comforts.

One final quirk is one I learned about since taking this journey is that I sing a lot. Some people have said I never stop singing. I sing when I am working on my laptop, while making coffee, while riding in vehicles, while waiting on the train, and while doing other things. Apparently, I sometimes sing too loudly, especially early in the morning, while taking a shower.

For years, I was afraid to sing.

As I mentioned earlier, people used to make fun of my singing. It's taken me a long time to believe those who say I'm a really good singer, and they love my voice. So, the idea that I might sing too much or too loudly is just wrong. Like everything else mentioned in this chapter, I'm working to get better. I don't really think my singing is truly a quirk; I think it's just that other people don't appreciate my musical stylings!

I hope you don't mind my sharing some of these observations that came from realizing that I always crumple up a water bottle. I'm sure you have some quirks, too. Maybe hearing me share mine will allow you to take a hard, honest look at your own annoying quirks. We all have them. Some of us are just lucky enough to live with people who love us enough to put up with them. If we are going to continue to strive to be better people, then eliminating them—or recognizing them and trying to eliminate them—from our lives is a critical part of that growth. I hope that gets you started thinking about how you can improve by changing some of those little things you do and have always done.

Key Takeaways:

We should try to recognize our annoying quirks and then eliminate them from our lives, to grow into better people.

It's important to be respectful of others.

Those who love us put up with our quirks, so we need to put up with theirs, too.

Chapter 25: Michele's House

Michele's house is a pretty large one that felt open and airy to me. It had a weird layout that took me a while to get used to. There was a glass top on the coffee table, and I had to learn where to set cups or bottles, so as not to leave a stain. We ate meals at her dining table, something we rarely do at my house. We usually take our meals in whatever chair we feel most comfortable in.

The living room was separate from the dining room, even though there weren't walls or doors involved in the separation, and I slept on her couch, even though she offered me a bed. I felt really comfortable on her couch.

Without being asked, I folded up my covers because that is something my mom and grandma taught me to do. I also cleaned up after myself because I could tell that her house wasn't the kind of place you left dirty dishes out. I respected her for that. Having kids and grandkids over often, it's probably not easy to keep clean. Plus, Michele also works—for the local school district.

I was nervous about using Michele's bathroom, for two reasons. One, being a big man, I've often had trouble with stopping up toilets by putting too much paper in them or not flushing as I went. I'm also never really sure which stuff in a bathroom is supposed to be used and what is just for decoration.

Also, going into a woman's bathroom, I was afraid of knocking things over, because trust me, you can never put them back exactly right—at least, I never have been able to. I'm also always conscious of potentially breaking other people's stuff. I do my best to be careful, but it's hard not seeing and also being kind of a large man. That was actually my biggest worry about using her bathroom.

On the way back to the kitchen or living room, I had to pass by a cabinet that was full of her treasures. I never asked what was in there, but judging by the doors, I assumed it was china. I was always veering to the right to make as sure as possible that I wouldn't run into it and destroy something just by bumping into it.

While I was there, we managed to have a good few days. She invited me to go swimming in their pool. I turned her down because of not having anything to swim in and because of the sore on my foot. I didn't want to potentially expose her kids to germs from a foot that might be infected.

Looking back, I wish I had gotten in the water and had fun with the rest of them. I could have worn my short pants in the pool.

Michele didn't have any computer equipment or printers in her living room. I don't recall finding dirty dishes in the sink. I think even the front of her refrigerator was smooth. They left me alone there a couple times, and I managed to figure out their TV remote. She also had Amazon Fire with Alexa, but I didn't play with it. I enjoyed it when Michael set it to play Sinatra music, and I got to hear a lot of great, old, big band swing music. I'm really a guy from another era when it comes to music and old-time radio.

Michele cooked some really good meals while I was there. Michael even cooked. He made pork kabobs.

We used to do an event in Groves, Texas, called the Texas State Pecan Festival. One of the favored vendors there was famous for his kabobs. We always tried to get him to tell us how he made them, but he would never tell us. Somehow, Michael figured out the secret ingredient. So, having kabobs like we used to look forward to having at Groves each year was a great experience.

While I was there, I had one funny thing happen.

I couldn't figure out or remember what drinks were in the refrigerator. I kept accidentally grabbing beer instead of soda. I couldn't bring myself to just pour it out, so I drank it. My brother told my mom about my drinking beer at his house and then at Michele's, so my mom was worried I was getting a drinking problem!

One of the times they left me by myself was when they took one of Wade's kids to a Little League baseball game. It was going to be hot and I wouldn't really have a way to follow the game, so I decided to stay behind. I wouldn't be able to see the game or have someone to do a play-by-play of each move, and they don't even keep score! In retrospect, maybe I missed out on something fun that day by staying at Michele's house in the air conditioning.

I got to talk with Michele quite a bit. I also got to observe her with her kids and grandkids. It was obvious just how much they loved each other and took care of each other. More importantly, you could tell they really liked each other and enjoyed being together.

One night, we all watched a movie. Michael's granddaughter was there, so it was a kids' movie. She picked *Troll Hunters*. At first, I thought, *Oh no, not a kids' movie!*

I remembered all the times I had watched movies like *Aladdin, Beauty and the Beast, The Little Mermaid*, etc., with Michael's and Michele's kids. I can admit to loving *Beauty and the Beast*. With the music in that movie, how could I not love it? But watching such movies on an endless loop had gotten old

168

(back when we were living, working, and traveling together) but I found myself getting into the music.

I was following the story, too, but the next thing I knew, I was waking up on the floor of the living room. Darn that sleep apnea! I'm going to have to watch that movie again, just to find out how it ends! That experience made me wish I could have become "the new me" sooner in life. Perhaps there would have been kids of my own instead of only nephews and nieces in my life.

Even Eva was a good family dog.

My niece, Dana, had gotten a new puppy. Like all new puppies, it was teething on everything. It even tried chewing on Eva. Eva, sensing she was dealing with a puppy, tolerated being used as a chew toy. Come to think of it, Penny was always really good with puppies or kittens. One time, we even found Penny playing with a young deer in our yard.

At one time, my mom, my dad, Patrick, Michael's family, and I shared a small house near Corpus Christi, Texas. We traveled together during the year, for a couple of seasons. I didn't really know what to do or how to be around all those young ones. I must admit that most of the time I was with Michael, Michele, and their kids, I wasn't very friendly. When Patrick's son, Seth, came along, he would eventually call me "un-fun Uncle Max." I think his calling me that helped me realize that I was too strict. I used to joke with people that I only knew words like "stop," "quit that," "don't," "no," and "I'm going to call your dad."

When I first knew Michele, she and the rest of us were living in a small, 900-square-foot home, which was actually a garage that was only partially converted. There was tension because of the number of people and the lack of space.

Michele once said, "I think your mom wanted you home but then didn't know what to do with you, once you were there."

Michele's children were young, back then. My niece, Shelby, almost said her first word because she thought I was going to run into her highchair. I came around the corner from the kitchen to the living room. Her chair hadn't been there before. She saw me coming and made as much noise as she could. I was able to stop and keep from running her over. I should mention that Michele's kids were tough, because for a few years, they lived in a house where the floors were concrete.

Even then, Michele was always trying to create a better and more orderly home. One day, she noticed they were replacing the carpets at a nearby department store. To her, it looked like the carpets they were tearing out were good enough to still be used in someone's home. So, she went to the store manager and asked him about having some of the soon-to-be-discarded carpeting. They offered to sell it to her at a reasonable price.

The manager even went so far as to tell her to see if she liked the color of the carpet that had been in the lingerie section. He told her that the lingerie section received the least foot traffic of any part of the store, which meant that the carpet from that section would have the most life left in it. I can't recall what color the carpet was, but it was so nice having it. That experience is another great example of what can happen when we find the courage to ask.

I feel like Michele and I finally got to know each other. I have a real respect for her and what she did—raising her kids pretty much on her own, for a lot of years.

I also believe we came to have the beginning of an understanding.

I gave her a copy of my first book, and I signed it "To a wonderful mom, a great host, and a real lady." We don't always make the best decisions the first time around. Sometimes, we screw it up royally and spend years being distant from each other. Then, we grow, and we learn more. We start to become the person we were meant to be.

I got to get to know Michele all over again, and when I left, I felt just as much concern for me as if we were family.

I'm tearing up a little as I write this. I have always wondered if my being there during the early years had strained my brother's marriage. I choose to believe that if anything, I was just one more obstacle for them, but it feels good to have cleared the air with my sister-in-law.

Whether she is actually married to Michael or not, I now think of her as my sister— something that didn't happen the first time around. I hope that will inspire you to believe that you can get a do-over.

You can mend those fences, even if you weren't the one who broke them down. Usually, it isn't one person or the other that creates the problem. Getting past situations like that usually starts by not worrying about whose fault it was and just trying to see each other as people.

I don't think it hurts any that none of us are in the carnival business anymore. Yes, I still help people sell amusement equipment. I get great satisfaction out of helping people sell rides or games they need to sell, but it's not the only way I make my living. It's not the same as operating a carnival or owning rides or games. Even though I earn money from that business, nowadays, my life is more about writing, speaking, coaching, and getting people booked on radio shows and podcasts.

Michael is driving a truck and selling on eBay and Michele works at the school, but they have time together on the weekends. Michele knows where Michael is and where he's going to be. He can be there for little league games, cookouts, days of swimming, and more. His income is so much more reliable than it ever was when he was a traveling-show painter or a carnival owner.

He has his house that is a mess that he lives in during the week, not that he's there much or does much living in it. She has an immaculate home that is warm and waiting for her kids and grandkids to come stay with her. There aren't any printers or car parts in her living room. Everything is where it ought to be in a clean, bright, inviting home. They aren't doing it the way that everyone says they should be, but they are happy. It really works for them.

I don't think I would want to follow their example. I still hope to find a woman half as special as Michele or my Aunt Paula or my own mom. (You will meet Paula in the next chapter.)

I can't wait to send Michele her copy of this book. In fact, I'm already trying to think of just the right words to write on it for her. She knew, all those years ago, that I didn't belong in the carnival. Of course, she probably didn't think any of us did. It's a hard way to make a living. She comes from a family where, for generations, husbands went to guaranteed jobs in manufacturing, and wives stayed home and ran the house. Things were way more predictable than they ever were for our carnival. Still, she did her best.

My dad always said there were showmen and carnies. He said the word "showman" implied class. He always encouraged me to aspire to be a showman. To me, it's the biggest compliment I can give someone. To me, Michele has become a real "show woman." I'm lucky to have had time with her and her family, during this trip. (Thanks, Michele.)

Key Takeaways:

You can mend fences and repair damaged relationships, even if you weren't the one who broke them, if you stop worrying about who caused the wreckage and simply tried to just see each other as people.

When you stay at someone else's home, offer to pitch in, whenever possible.

Chapter 26: Missed Trains

When I left on my first Amtrak adventure in December 2016, there were some people who wondered if I would make it back home. Some feared I would never return home again because I'd get sucked up by the vast Amtrak train system. So, I thought I'd share two different experiences from my first speaking and signing trip that proved my beliefs about Amtrak.

I felt like they would look after me and make sure I got where I needed to go. That was certainly true of my New York City trip. Back then, being the winner of their prestigious award, I was a VIP—a celebrity— who was traveling first-class. This time, I was a regular person traveling coach.

When you place your booking, they ask if you are disabled, among other things that might get you a discount. Once they know you are disabled, they put that on your ticket and notifications are sent along the way to alert people that you will need assistance.

On this particular trip, I was forgotten on a train twice. Once was partly my fault. The other was caused by the car attendant being distracted.

The first time it happened, I was going into Philadelphia. The train was quite a bit late, and I was tired. I wasn't paying close enough attention to the announcements. Plus, there was a woman who was traveling with her grandson. He was so excited about soon seeing his father again that he was bouncing in his seat and even dancing in the aisle. I couldn't blame him. Also, Amtrak employees have always been so good about coming and getting me that when they asked for passengers getting off in Philadelphia to move to the front of the car, I honestly didn't think they meant me.

Once they realized my error, they set about finding the quickest way to get me back to Philly. They called ahead to Trenton, New Jersey. The people there were alerted to help me get turned around and back to my destination, which was actually pretty easy, considering that I was in what they call the Northeastern Corridor. That's the part of the country with the highest number of train routes and the best quality of engines and tracks.

I had approximately a 90-minute delay before catching my next train, so I had a soda and had a nice conversation with the agent while I waited for it. There was a lot going on in that station—lots of music and smells of great foods. I wished I had had more time there. The agent congratulated me for not being one of those excitable types of people who would get hysterical over such a situation. I told him that part of it is just knowing or having faith that I can depend on the people at Amtrak to help look after me. Some people would be too independent to think that way or to say that out loud, even if they do.

The second time it happened was when I was going to Raleigh on my way to visit my Aunt Paula and other members of the Ivey family in Spartanburg, South Carolina. The car attendant had come by a minute or two before arriving in the station, to tell me that he would come get me after everyone else had gotten off. He got busy with a group of Boy Scouts in the next car and forgot about me. I think he said there were over 30 of them. He couldn't have apologized more.

They checked where I wanted to go against the train schedules in the area. They found out that if I got off in Rocky Mount, North Carolina, I could catch the train I wanted, although a couple of stops earlier.

They told me if I had my heart set on being in Raleigh, they would send me back in a taxi, at their expense.

They also gave me a free cup of coffee.

That particular mistake worked out for me, for three reasons.

One, the time I spent waiting to catch my next train was much less than the layover I would have had if I had caught the correct train to start with. The second reason is that we decided to change my route so that I could get off in Charlotte, which was much closer to where my Aunt Paula lived.

The third is that I was able to have my weekly Bible study with my teacher, Jon Beck, because the station was so sparsely populated. Besides me, there only two other people were there.

Jon first tried calling me on my phone. That didn't work, so he tried me on Skype. I hadn't used Skype on my new tablet yet, so I had to install it and update the password.

Once I started studying the Bible more, it became important to me not to miss my Bible study or weekly meetings, unless absolutely necessary.

Since the Jehovah's Witnesses believe in making our meetings as available as possible, each congregation broadcasts their meetings over one of those free conference call systems. That way, people who are sick, elderly, or disabled can still get their spiritual food, so to speak. My faith and my congregation are a part of my story, so I felt this was the best place to mention this. I'm not perfect. I make mistakes, but I'm doing my best to follow the Bible's teachings.

Back on my way to South Carolina, I was happy to be back on the train. As I've mentioned before, Amtrak doesn't splurge on furniture in their stations, except maybe for the business-class or first-class lounges in major cities. Thankfully, the seats on the trains are very comfortable, even in coach. They are nothing like the cramped confines of planes or buses. If I hadn't already had confidence in the people at Amtrak, I do now.

I hope my experiences will remind you that there are a lot of good people in this world who will help out, when needed or when asked. Some are employees and wear uniforms. Others are just truly nice people who genuinely want to help, and will, if you let them. I also hope that knowing this will give you courage to step out in your own life. Maybe you would like to come along on my next trip. I'm always on the lookout for someone as crazy as I am who is ready for an adventure!

Key Takeaways:

Some mistakes are blessings in disguise.

There are a lot of people who truly want to and will help you.

Chapter 27: Having Style

One thing I learned from my extended Amtrak adventure is that not all stations are the same.

Some are open 24 hours, where people can come and go as they wish, as long as they have a ticket or are going to buy one. Some are open 24 hours, but they are locked down during the night, not allowing you to come or go, once the doors are closed. There are some that are only open long enough for people to board a train or get off of an arriving train, and there are even some that actually have no station at all—they are pretty much just a siding with some fencing. The latter was the case in Spartanburg, South Carolina.

I have to thank my Aunt Paula and her husband, Mark, for coming to get me in Charlotte. It meant a bit of a car ride for them, but it avoided them having to pick me up in Spartanburg at five in the morning. I was very happy they made the offer, and I didn't hesitate in the least to say yes.

During my visit, Paula ended up helping me do more to remake my image. She was actually pretty sneaky about it. As a woman,

I think she knew I would balk if she told me her plans in advance. So, maybe she planned things, and maybe she didn't. Either way, I'm thankful for what she did.

First, she talked me into going swimming in her pool. She said I looked really pale and needed to get some sun on my face. I had fun splashing around with her son, Jaxon, and I felt much recovered from my travels for it.

Then, she noticed my eyebrows needed to be trimmed—a common problem for me. I usually have it done when I get my hair cut, but I had been traveling and had let my hair grow out. After my experience in Buffalo, I realized that my hair was nice and curly and looked good long. So, Paula trimmed my eyebrows for me. She went a bit farther by plucking a few hairs from above my nose.

Next, she dyed my hair. She had taken a photo of me swimming and playing in the pool with Jaxon, then and posted it online, and apparently, several people commented on the grey in my hair and how old it made me look.

One morning, she told me she was going out to buy toilet paper at the dollar store. She came back and said, "Hey, Maxi, look what they had on sale." Paula and the other Iveys have always called me Maxi because my dad and I shared the same first name. She told me the hair dye only cost three bucks. It seemed like a fortuitous event.

Since starting my transformation several years ago, I've become much more open to seeing events as experiences. It doesn't matter how big or small an opportunity may seem, they are all meant to be enjoyed. So, when she mentioned having the hair dye, I thought, *Why the heck not let her dye my hair?*

She shampooed my hair and eyebrows with the mixture. She left it on until the timer said to wash it out. She then used the conditioner on it.

After she was through, she said it looked so much better, and I looked much younger, more vital, and even more successful. She said I now looked more like the kind of guy people would pay big bucks to hire as their coach.

Afterward, she said, "Let's have some fun with it."

So, she rubbed some gunk in her hands and swirled my hair around, like she was mixing a stew. She spiked some of my hair up. She had me sit in the living room, straddling a chair backwards. Then, she tried me in some different poses. Next, she put sunglasses on me and pronounced that I should wear sunglasses all the time because they gave definition to my face. Following that, she found a hat. She tried it all together and said that it made a great new look.

We took some photos and posted them online as a slide show. For the background music, I chose "Rock Star" by Nickelback. I was proud of how I looked and all the compliments I got from my friends and family online. *Darn, why didn't I think to ask her if I could have the hat and sunglasses?*

Here is a picture of me straddling the chair, with sunglasses on:

Here is a picture of me straddling the chair, wearing both the sunglasses and a hat:

At first, I was worried about my ability to maintain the new look, but several friends have told me that I would have no trouble finding someone locally to touch up my hair every month or so.

They also said that I could learn how to style it when I had occasions where I needed to look like the rock star I was becoming.

One friend suggested I could even get a hotel employee to help out in a pinch.

Another friend said, "Max, as you get more famous, you can start hiring someone to meet you in whatever city you are in and have them fix it up professionally." But then, the look itself is kind of haphazard and messy.

When Paula saw those comments, she said, "If you ever need someone to style your hair for an event, you better call me first!"

Then she laughed and added, "Just tell them they have to provide your stylist with a plane ticket and a hotel room."

Paula is a very adventurous person.

She has often taken weekend trips to New York City or Washington, D.C., and she is one of those people who it's really hard to say no to. Her zest for life and spirit of adventure is infectious.

In fact, she is the only one to have ever talked me into riding the Ferris wheel. I may have grown up in a family of carnival owners, but I've never been crazy about heights or anything where I have to turn upside down!

Paula also said that I had too much hair on my back. She promised or threatened to shave it for me.

I'm not sure if she was serious. I understand some men are so hairy that they need to have it shaved or waxed. To me, that just seems a little too much, especially as I'm always wearing a suit or at least a shirt and tie when speaking or appearing at events.

Next, she told me that a friend of hers had lost weight and was going to give away some of his clothes. He was supposed to have some dress shirts. Paula got him to come by her house so I could try them on.

She found two that she liked a lot. They fit a little tight on me, mainly in the shoulders. Paula said I could wear them over a T-shirt. She said that lots of people wear them that way now—they wear an unbuttoned dress shirt over a T-shirt. She then bought me two new lightweight T-shirts to go with them.

Finally, she took me to her favorite hair stylist and had her cut my hair. She left most of the length but trimmed it up so it looked cleaner.

Paula and her friend suggested it was almost long enough to put in a ponytail and asked me if I would ever consider that. I told them I wasn't sure I was ready to go that far. I think I remember them saying something about feathering. Either way, it's still easy for everyday use. I just comb it straight back.

I have to wash it and comb it a lot more often, but I like my hair. At my age, I'm happy to say I have a full head of hair. I never thought about having the grey removed. It actually goes against something my dad taught me.

If you have followed me for any length of time, you've probably already heard me tell this story, but I'm going to tell it again, just in case you haven't. When I was in my teens, I started getting grey hair, mainly on the right-front side. I complained to my dad about having grey hair at such a young age.

He said, "Son, the Ivey men either go grey or go bald, but they never do both. So, if I were you, I'd thank God for those grey hairs."

The funny thing is that when he got into his 50s, he used to use that stuff called Grecian Formula to remove the grey from his hair. I would never think of him as having been vain, but wanted to look good.

He never dressed real fancy. He always used to say that a carnival owner with sharp clothes would make the fair and festival committee people wonder about how you can afford to dress so sharp. To borrow a phrase, he did "clean up good," or so I'm told. I like to think that he would approve of my new look. He might not care for the spiky hair, sunglasses, or the hat, but he'd appreciate the show business aspect of me needing to look like the rock star that people are starting to think of me as being.

My look has improved even more since the initial writing of this book because I had a complete makeover in June 2018 by a professional stylist, Chelsea Nguyen. I will be sharing the stories and experiences surrounding these events in my next book, which will be the third book in my travel series (but my fifth book)!

I can't wait to stand on a stage again, hear someone give me a great introduction, and have them play my music. The only thing is my theme song is "The River" by Garth Brooks, definitely not rock and roll music, although Garth has often been credited (or blamed) for combining country and rock. So, maybe some rock music when I'm introduced and me singing "The River," like my friend and speaking mentor, Azuka Zuke, suggested having at the conclusion of my talks.

Key Takeaways:

Be open to changing your hair and/or clothing style, because it may be just the improvement you need to look more successful!

Even though looks are not everything, having an improved look will help you feel better.

Chapter 28: Aunt Francis

I was really happy I got to see my Aunt Francis. Before I talk about that, I want to give you some background information.

I had met her many years ago. She had come to visit us during the summer and actually traveled with the carnival. More than that, she turned out to be an awesome person and a great worker. She didn't mind the heat or long hours and was great with the customers. You didn't have to tell her to call people in, which means asking the people passing by your booth if they want to play your game. She worked in the balloon-dart game where they would pop balloons to win mirrors. She kept the balloons blown up, the darts picked up, and the mirrors sleeved up. If you've never heard of that, it means the mirrors would be kept in paper sleeves.

I spent quite a bit of time with Aunt Francis, talking and watching TV. Luckily for me, my grandma had watched the same soap operas, so I at least knew the names of most of the characters and the general family lines. Since soaps are very slow-moving in the plot department, I was able to catch up pretty quickly.

I'm funny that way. Even if I don't care for a show, I can become interested in it. It becomes kind of a challenge to see how quickly I can pick up the storylines. Other times, I just have to admit that I'm easily entertained. One of the people who read for me in college once told me that in my case, TV was the root of all evil. I told her I thought money was the root of all evil. I added, "For such a big tree, it must need more than one root."

Aunt Francis and I had similar tastes in movies and TV shows. We would often hang out in the motel while others were making trips, moving the rides, setting them up, or taking them down.

When the carnival was open, she worked the game on the other side of my game trailer. My dad put her in that game because he always wanted the most responsible and attentive person to watch out for me while I was working my duck pond. So, Aunt Francis would keep people from ripping me off, tell me what bill people were giving me, and sometimes run in the back of the trailer to fetch more stock.

I want to tell you about my duck pond game, mainly because it fits right into my "finding solutions" approach.

Even with an attentive partner in the next booth, people would still try to cheat. We knew that would happen when we were putting the game together and writing the numbers on the ducks, which is called "framing the joint."

My game was what is called a "build-up" or an "add-them-up" duck pond, meaning people would add the numbers on the bottom of their ducks together to win a prize. They could also combine multiple games together, to win a better prize.

Every carnival game for kids is supposed to have at least one grand-prize-winning tag or number in it, but we decided that in my pond, we would leave that out, just to make it fair. So, in my duck pond, there were only so many points someone could get from each set of ducks.

Now, I want to emphasize that this isn't common, especially not now in the more corporate version of the carnival midway.

We only had an eight-ride carnival with four games. Even so, I always had good prizes in the game. Even someone who picked up low-numbered ducks would win a decent prize, and I always counted slowly so the customer could count their own ducks along with me.

Knowing that there wasn't any way someone could pay one dollar and win a ten-dollar prize gave me the freedom to not have to worry about whether people were cheating or not. The funny thing is, my dad knew that, too.

He helped me figure out how many of each numbered duck to put in the pond. However, while I'd ignore the punk kids that cheated, my dad would get mad about it. More than once, my brother, Patrick, had to calm him down.

Another interesting thing is that more than once, the festival organizers would hear about my duck pond and come play it for themselves. I can't tell you how many times I said, "You get a prize every time. Just come pick up the lucky ducks." I still have one of the ducks from the last pond I ever worked.

Those are good memories, and Aunt Francis was a big part of one of the best summers I ever had in the business. When you have good company, good weather, and good money, it's easy to be happy.

Some weeks, we did really well. Others, there would be very few people on the midway, and we would just sit there and talk. We would always eat. That was something my dad believed in.

I think almost all the Iveys and a good number of my mom's family (the Wagners) can eat heartily. My dad used to joke that he would defy people to find any pictures in the family photo albums where someone wasn't holding a spoon or fork. When things aren't going well, and you have lots of time to kill, you eat. At least, we did. If my dad wasn't bringing us food from the booths set up at the event, Francis would be sharing Vienna sausages, crackers, and other stuff with me.

I used to like riding with Aunt Francis on the jumps because she never left a town without loading up on water, soft drinks, and non-perishable food. If you got stuck on the side of the road with her, you were going to be prepared. The other thing I loved about her that year was how she approached life. Her idea was no matter what you were doing, there was a way to find enjoyment in it.

She also gave me one of my best memories.

It was because of her that I drank beer in front of my dad. We ordered pizza one night. She either went to the store or insisted my dad go. She told him there was no way she was going to eat pizza without beer. She said it just wasn't right. I had one beer before switching to milk, but that was still a milestone.

My dad preached about the problems that come from drinking. I think he's partly the reason why I never drank much. So, to drink a beer in front of him without any fear of a whipping or at least him yelling at me was a big deal.

Now that you know why I wanted to see her again, I'll tell you about her.

Aunt Francis was 82 at the time of this writing, and was proud of it. She told me she had no reason to lie about her age, as she earned every year. (Since I had seen her, she broke a hip and had a minor stroke. With physical therapy, she healed, although she moves a little slower. Another update about her will be included a bit later.) Her mind was perfectly clear and she was still just as sharp as ever. She was also still just as vibrant and feisty in her personality.

Aunt Paula told her about my book, and I showed her a copy. She asked me about buying one. I told her what I usually charged. She explained that with being on a fixed income, she couldn't pay that. I asked her what she could pay.

She asked me, "What about five dollars?"

I told her sure and I autographed the book for her. I was really happy to do that.

I would have probably given her the book, but you can never tell about what may have happened if I did. As a rule, the Iveys are pretty independent people, and I worried about offending her if I had offered it for free. I told her about my trip to New York City and that I had hoped to have another book out by the time my next trip east had started.

Here are two pictures of me with my Aunt Francis, who is holding my first book:

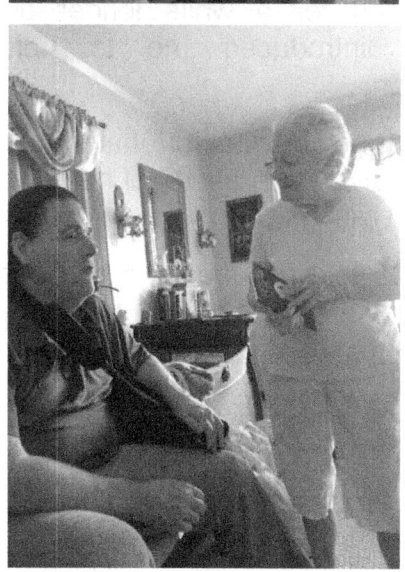

My Aunt Paula, my Aunt Francis, and I enjoyed chatting together.

We reminisced about my Grandma Pearl, who had also been a lively person until late in life.

Grandma Pearl never wanted to have us call her Grandma. She just didn't see herself as old.

Then, someone mentioned social media.

I said, "Yeah, Grandma Pearl was always at the center of everything, and if she were still alive, she would be like one of the Kardashians. She would rule Facebook—at least, in South Carolina."

We talked for a while longer and Aunt Francis introduced me to her great-grandson.

She told me she was fortunate to be able to say that five generations of her family were alive at that time.

She also told me that she has one of the family order her books from Amazon. (Yes, at her age, she is still reading actual books!)

Just before I left, Paula took some pictures of me and Aunt Francis.

I didn't remember her being so short or tiny.

Here is a picture of me with my Aunt Francis:

Visiting my Aunt Francis was one of the real highlights of my visit to Jonesville. I didn't know it at the time, but that visit would be the last time I saw her. She passed away before this book was published.

Key Takeaways:

When you have good company, good weather, and good money, it's easy to be happy.

Remember your loved ones and take time to reminisce because good memories will also make you happy.

Chapter 29: Picking and Singing

One of my favorite memories from my first speaking and signing trip was totally spontaneous. It happened while I was visiting with Aunt Paula and her family.

I hadn't been back to South Carolina since before my dad's death. I hadn't seen many of my aunts, uncles, or cousins in over 30 years. I didn't have a lot of notice, so I wasn't expecting a big reunion or anything. The Saturday night before I left to come back home, several things came together.

First, my Uncle Vernon had just bought the home up the street from Paula's and had picked that week to bring his furniture and move in. He brought several other members of the family to help unload and carry everything in.

So, there was Uncle Vernon and his wife, Pam. There was Uncle Terry and his wife, Betty Sue. There was my cousin, Jay Ivey, who is, as I later found out, a classically trained opera singer and teacher. I can't remember who else was there. Being blind, I couldn't see everybody. It had also been years since I had seen those family members.

After they unloaded the moving truck, we all gathered at tables around Mark and Paula's pool. Paula had put together some food for everyone. There was beer and soft drinks. Vernon got out a guitar, and we sat around, singing all the songs everyone knew. The guitar was a total piece of junk, but Vernon made it sound great. Plus, it was more about enjoying each other's company than the sound of the guitar or our voices.

That night, Vernon told me a big secret about performing.

He said, "Max, when I don't know the words, I make them up. As long as I sing them as if I know them, most people won't even care. If you want a real laugh, listen to the reactions when I play songs by Freddy Fender and sing the Spanish parts. People think I am singing it just like he did, but who knows what I'm singing some nights?"

He proved this by singing a song called "Shotgun Car," a song my dad wrote as a teenager.

I have a video of Vernon and some friends of his playing the song. Everyone wanted to hear him sing my dad's song.

He finally agreed but only after saying, "I'm going to sing this song, but I may not sing it exactly like I did on the video." That reminded me of a story my dad once told me.

My dad said, "Max, me and some of my relatives had a band when we were in high school. We would play the bars and perform for tips. They didn't know the words to a lot of the songs people requested. One time, a man offered us a dollar to play a song, and I replied, 'We only know the first verse, so will you take that, for a quarter?'"

I really miss my dad.

I'm glad I didn't know just how talented Jay is, or I might have been self-conscious. Paula played some of his YouTube videos the next day, after he was gone. Jay teaches at Jacksonville University, I think it is.

I sang right along with the rest of them. This is important, because if you haven't been following me for long, you don't know about my struggles with singing in public.

Vernon also told me that I sounded a lot like my dad. Being a daddy's boy, this was great to hear. I am one of those people who has trouble singing out loud unless he knows all the words. Or at least I have to have someone next to me who I can count on to know them, so I can at least cheat off of them.

At one point, Paula asked me to sing one of my favorites. I don't know why I chose "One Good Well" by Don Williams instead of "The River" by Garth Brooks. I don't know why I didn't sing both. Vernon did his best to play along, but it was probably the first time he had played that song. Paula actually suggested that I sing the song I had sung in Buffalo.

Later, I had to wonder if Paula had planned everything, knowing I was coming. I even wonder if she had told Vernon to expect me to sing "The River." I wouldn't put it past Paula to have organized the event without telling me. She is that kind of person. She really believes in the value of family, and she had to know it would be a while before I would be back that way again. I just wish I had taken the hint. I would've loved to have had a video of me and Vernon doing "The River"!

I will admit to having four or five beers and eating a little more than I should have. It was the perfect end to a day that started with swimming in their pool and getting some sun, followed by listening to a NASCAR race on the radio.

I share this partly because it is a favorite memory but more because I want to remind you that in whatever we do, we have to take time to enjoy experiences like these. Don't be so focused on your mission that you miss out on some great experience.

I won't claim to be perfect in this area. For example, when I left Buffalo, I had found out that ZZ Top was going to do a free concert in the park. Al and I could have gone. I know he would have taken me, but I was focused on making the train I had booked to head on to Florida. I actually could have pushed that ticket back a couple of days. I had enough notice, but I was suffering from tunnel vision. I was too determined to get on that train and head to the next town. I wonder if I would have made a different decision if I hadn't been traveling solo.

When I told my cousin, Bobbie Gayle, about that, she replied that if she had been with me, there is no way we would have missed that free concert. If you read my third book, which is actually the first one in my travel series, *The Blind Blogger's NYC Adventures*, about my first trip to New York and my first Amtrak experience, then you know Bobbie Gayle—or Beep, as we call her—is another one of those people who knows how to enjoy life. You know, I think that may be genetic on the Ivey side of the family, now that I think of it.

Why did I stick so tightly to the schedule? There was no other reason than pure stubbornness and a desire to stick to a plan.

I'm hoping you can learn from my mistakes and my successes in this area.

I had fun hanging out with my family, and I would have had fun at that concert. The funny thing is, you would think I would have carried that lesson with me from New York City. I generally enjoy every moment, regardless of whether or not anyone else would deem the experience exciting. I've written about this subject, and I do my best to teach others. However, like I often say, the most important lessons in life usually have to be relearned, from time to time. It was that way again on my first speaking and signing trip, in the area of money. I hope to avoid backsliding in such areas in the future, but I'm honest enough to admit that I won't be surprised if this isn't the last time I write about these topics.

Key Takeaways:

Don't be so focused on your mission that you miss out on some great experience.

Take time to enjoy every experience.

We sometimes need to relearn important lessons.

Chapter30: New Shoes... Almost

Paula's help didn't end with improving my style. She also did her best to help me with the sore that was still plaguing my left foot.

When I first got to her house, she looked at my foot and said it scared her. She said it was swollen, and the color made her think of a diabetic with circulation issues. I assured her that I had an A1C test done as part of the regular follow-up to my gastric surgery. I also told her that my podiatrist had run a uric acid test, ruling out gout. A check of my circulation showed the pulse in both ankles was strong and regular. Still, she was so worried that she took a photo and sent it to one of my cousins, who works at a doctor's office. The response was that it looked bad, but if my doctors weren't concerned, then we shouldn't worry.

But Paula doctored my foot. She cut away some of the remainder of the large scab that had been on it.

I had been going to a podiatrist, Doctor Miles, every other week for a few months. He would remove more and more of the callus and advise me on proper wound care. I told her Dr. Miles and the emergency room docs who originally treated it told me to always cover it with antibiotic ointment, a bandage, socks, and shoes, but she thought leaving the sore open to the air would help it heal better.

I listened to Paula, and we left it uncovered. I then felt bad for Paula because she had to keep wiping up spots of blood from her floor.

Paula lives in a beautiful home. Unlike ours, it has central air and heat, meaning there are those metal grates sprinkled throughout the house. I kept dinging my foot on those and re-injuring it, so eventually, I accepted her suggestion to let her lead me whenever I wanted to go, from one room to another. It was weird to have to accept that, but it kept me from knocking the sore on those sharp edges.

I told Paula about my shoes not fitting good enough to wear for any length of time. She told me that until my foot was completely healed, I needed new shoes. She further pointed out that now would be the perfect time to shop for them. She said if I bought them when my left foot was swollen, that I would know they will fit and not risk hurting my foot in the future. So, we went shopping.

Paula took me to several stores. We started in a church-run resale place that everyone in her area just calls "the Jesus store." It's one of those places that sells new and used items. No one really knows the name of the store anymore. We couldn't find anything suitable, so we went to a couple of actual shoe stores and looked some more. I kept trying different types of shoes on, hoping for a good fit, but I didn't have any luck. With my flat feet and my foot being a bit swollen, most shoes we tried on just weren't long enough or wide enough.

We almost found one pair—a boot-type shoe, from a company called Alegria. I loved the feel of them, and she loved the look of them. The shoes usually sell for $175 but were on sale for $50. If they had had a 15 wide, they would have been perfect. Paula said she would leave her name and number with the store clerk in case they got a larger pair of those shoes in stock. We went to the official website for Alegria shoes and also to Amazon but only found much smaller sizes of the shoes for sale. I am known for having trouble spending money on myself, but I could actually see spending that kind of money if I found a pair that fit really good.

Mark and Paula's son, Jaxon, and daughter, Courtney, were also very nice to me. Jaxon gave up his bedroom, which meant that when I was using it, he also gave up his video game console. Jaxon was a cool young guy—a big-time pro wrestling fan in love with Shawn Michaels (one of the old-time wrestlers)—and he talked me into watching *Cars 3* with him. Again, I was skeptical about watching a kids' movie, but Disney snuck a lot of self-help messages into the storyline, and the ending was surprising and encouraging because of the message it sends to young girls.

Courtney was a high school student who was in the middle of the preparations to go off to college—a time that I understand is a big deal between a mother and daughter—and I was intruding on that time, but she was friendly to me nonetheless.

I overheard her talk about how some of her high school friends weren't right for her anymore. She was talking about how they were friends because they went to the same school in the small town of Jonesville.

I shared a line from the movie *Armageddon*. In there, Bruce Willis tells his daughter that her choice for a husband wasn't a choice, it was a lack of options.

While staying at Paula's, I woke up early one morning, needing to go to the bathroom. While in there, the chain that connects the plunger to the handle in the toilet came loose, and the water kept running and running. I didn't want to wake anyone up, so I tried to fix it myself. It had happened to me before, and I figured I could just reconnect that chain and go back to bed. So, I picked up the lid to the back of their big, oversized toilet, which meant that the lid was a huge, heavy piece of porcelain. I tried holding it with one hand while trying to hook the chain back with the other but that didn't work, so I put the toilet lid down. Yet, I still couldn't get that chain hooked back up.

Eventually, Paula came and she got Mark to fix it. She wasn't mad, but she pointed out that I could have done a lot of damage to the porcelain and should have never tried to fix it myself. I can see her point and I now laugh when I think of myself with the lid in one hand and my body twisted around, trying to fix that toilet chain.

I finally had to leave Paula's, to head back to Houston, but before I could leave, I had to wait for a new client, to pay his latest invoice. It was nice knowing that I had earned the money to pay for that final ticket home while traveling. I knew he would pay me, which he did.

Paula and Mark loaded me up for the ride to the Amtrak pickup station in Spartanburg.

You know how I mentioned earlier that some towns have only a tiny place to wait on the train? Well, that's Spartanburg. So, we sat in her truck with the motor running, at five in the morning, in a really bad part of town. In fact, Mark asked Paula if they should both carry their guns when walking me to the train. Paula said no one would know.

Before I knew it, I had my ticket in hand, a bag full of snacks, and was—sadly—on my way back home.

I really miss my Aunt Paula and her husband, Mark. They are great people—a couple who also truly love each other and their kids. Mark took me into his house because I was Paula's family, not knowing how long I would stay, how much of a fuss they would need to make, or how much I might eat. They just never seemed to worry about it.

Maybe next time, I'll be lucky enough to have Paula go on an adventurous trip with me.

Paula really opened my eyes to the importance of my personal appearance. She also reminded me to continue living life as if everything is an experience to be treasured.

As a result of my foot problems, I've learned that you can't skimp on your feet. As a matter of fact, that thought stayed with me all the way home, to the point that maybe I was praying for better shoes. I say this because of something that happened in the New Orleans terminal. On the way home, I once again found myself sleeping on a green plastic chair. I still couldn't bring myself to pay for a whole night in a motel for the seven hours I would need it. In the morning, while I was waiting to board the train to Houston, a lady came up to me with a problem. Her suitcase was over the weight limit for checking the bag. She was going to have to leave some things behind. The one thing she said she wouldn't miss was what I was told looked like a brand new pair of size 14 Timberland boots.

I tried the left one on. I thought to myself, *If they fit, I would just throw my shoes away.* I had actually thrown away my black shoes in South Carolina, on the advice of Aunt Paula, and I was down to just the one pair of rather old tennis shoes that I wouldn't have missed. I think the right boot would have fit, but the left one was too tight and would have rubbed my pinky toe raw. But I thought about it hard.

Eventually, the woman had to just leave them. One of the other people in the terminal told her that despite the safety inside, the neighborhood was pretty rough outside. They suggested that if the woman just left those shoes outside the station, someone would take them, regardless of fit, so that's what she did.

If your feet hurt, everything else hurts.

My friend, Cassandra, who drives me to church, told me that if your shoes don't fit, it can affect your mental health. I told her about all the trouble I had with my feet on my first speaking and signing trip that was mainly caused by my shoes. She asked what I thought the problem was. I told her that I realized that I had never worn those shoes for extended periods of time. I explained that I had always put them on to go to church or the doctor's office and then took them off as soon as I was home.

She said, "Oh, they weren't all-day shoes, only three-hour shoes."

I must have looked at her funny.

She added, "Well, you wouldn't know this because you are a guy, but women have one-hour, two-hour, and three-hour shoes. It's okay as long as you know this and don't try to wear your three-hour ones all day."

She never laughed at me, but I got the feeling it was a near thing.

Still, I learned a valuable lesson about feet, shoes, and finding that pair or pairs that look good and that you can wear all day, if necessary. I have written about the importance of good health to success in life and business but I mistakenly never thought about this in reference to my feet. I won't make the mistake again. Even if I find a good comfortable pair or two of dressy shoes, when traveling, I'll still wear my tennis shoes or maybe even some boots.

Key Takeaways:

Live life as if everything is an experience to be treasured.

Having comfortable shoes on your feet is vital to good health as well as your success.

Chapter 31: My Key Takeaways and Next Steps

It's important to tell you what I was thinking and feeling when I left on my first speaking and signing trip, because I want you to realize that while I wasn't feeling actual fear, I was working through a lot of uncertainty.

My younger brother, Patrick, had suffered a heart attack in January 2017. He had been in the hospital for a long time and had only recently returned to work. My second book, *It's Not the Cookie, It's the Bag: An Easy-to-Follow Guide to Weight Loss Success*, had not sold well. I wasn't bringing in much from amusement equipment sales on the Midway Marketplace. I still only had one regular-paying client for my online publicity services. So, money was really tight. I had a hard time taking the $500 I did have and spending it on this trip. In addition, I only had one bona fide event—my talk at DreamCon in Philadelphia, which didn't come with a speaking fee. I was hoping that my appearance there would result in some book sales.

Prior to leaving on this trip, I had been talking with my friend, Al Chase, about his getting me a book signing or speaking gig in Buffalo, and he was working on it. I had spoken with another friend in Raleigh at the Governor Morehead School for the Blind. We had a tentative arrangement for me to come give a talk to the students there. She was pretty confident she could also book me an event in the city, independent from the school. So, to be honest, I was leaving on a six-week trip mostly on spec. As it turned out, those events didn't happen. Talks couldn't get booked and neither could additional book signings.

I picked my return date because of some doctor appointments that would start on June 27th, 2017. I thought, *Why not stay gone as long as possible and see what happens?* However, as I prepared to get on the train, I thought, *Max, what the hell are you doing? You don't really have this money to spend. You should give it to your mom and let her spend it on groceries or the electric bill or something.* I also thought, *Heck, what will you do if you can't book additional events?*

I then asked myself, *What's going to happen if you don't sell books? What if no other money shows up, like it has in the past?*

I was really starting to scare myself.

These thoughts plagues me until I remembered who I am. It helped that my brother, Patrick, told me not to worry about the money. It also helped that I had friends and family who had offered to host me in their homes. Other than paying for a motel room during my first weekend out, I knew my expenses would be very low. I reminded myself, *You've been talking about this online for weeks now. You need to do this. What would all those people think if you chickened out? If you backed down, what would it mean to those people who see you as an inspiration and someone who does crazy scary things, even when he is honestly scared about doing them?* I also reminded myself that if I could make it to New York City and survive there by myself for two weeks, I had nothing to be afraid of.

I thought the same God who looked after me in the past would look after me in the future. Prior to leaving, I noticed that my family was starting to get excited about my going. They were helping me buy clothes and fussing over my need for a haircut. They were asking me where I would stay, who I would live with, and how long I would be gone. They were asking if I would get to visit my friend in Pennsylvania, who I talked to most Fridays as part of my over-the-phone mastermind group.

As you know, I went, despite my uncertainties and doubts, and I had an amazing trip.

There were some scary moments, but thanks to friends and family, I was never in any real danger. I always had a place to stay, food to eat, and a ride if I needed to go somewhere.

I hope you are now thinking to yourself, *If Max can do this, then what is my excuse? If he can go off on a six-week trip by himself, with only a few hundred bucks in his pocket, then why can't I?*

My entire experience is proof that there is no perfect time. I could have looked at my circumstances and told myself, *Max, this is crazy, even for you, so stay home.* Instead, I decided to go out my front door and depend on myself, my creativity, my friends, and my family, with the belief that somehow, some way, my trip would be amazing.

I enjoyed every experience, from swimming on a hot, bright, sunny day to speaking at DreamCon to sitting on a back porch, singing with my family, to visiting Niagara Falls.

I hope this is another example to you that life's adventures are always more successful and enjoyable if you approach them with the childlike wonder of a six-year-old making their first trip to Disneyland.

I really hope this book inspires you to not only plan but also actually go off on your own big adventure.

If you are an author or speaker, then get out there and share your story. If you are a musician, then find a place to play and sing where people can hear you. If you are an artist, then take photos of your work and submit them to a magazine or show them to a gallery owner. If you want to learn to fly, then head out to the airport and see if someone offers lessons.

It won't always be easy. Heck, most of the time, especially in the beginning, it will probably be hard as hell. But you have to start. You have to take those steps and take those risks. The great stories come from those of us willing to try, willing to get hurt, willing to look silly, and willing to succeed—because it takes real heart and guts to be willing to risk enough to succeed.

I hope you will learn a lot from my sharing this first speaking and signing tour of mine. I know I'm getting a lot from sharing it. I'm paying those people back who encouraged me when I needed it most. I'm showing gratitude for my success and already planning my next big adventure. I don't know for sure what it is yet. I'm thinking it may be a national tour to promote the book about my New York City trip. We'll see.

I've joked that I should call my first national tour "The Trains, Buses, Taxis, and Uber Tour." I have become concerned about the future of Amtrak, something I love. I have offered to be an ambassador for their company and to testify before Congress. So far, they have turned me down.

I am always sending out emails and meeting new people online. I have sent out prayers and actual requests to speakers I respect about someday sharing a stage with them. I have talked to people about putting on a "No Excuses" conference or virtual summit. So far, none of these has really captured my imagination or passion.

I like to tell people they should never put limits on God. He usually has dreams for us bigger than anything we can contemplate. So, I'm waiting to see what is in store for me next. This whole trip started when I got an email inviting me to come to Philadelphia and give a talk about dreams and dreamers. I can't wait to see what this next big thing will be.

Now, you can see why I always say that I get up every morning expecting something great to happen. I know that there will be something positive, every day. It may be an event, an experience, or a special person. That is why I also look forward to checking my email first thing in the morning. I've been told it's not good for me, but I just can't wait to find that one great email that will get me off on the right foot for the whole day.

So, let's get going together. I can't wait to find out what is next—both for me and for you. I look forward to getting an email telling me about your adventure. They don't all have to be big ones. Don't forget, you have to take those small steps. I'm wishing you an amazing new activity, interest, or adventure in your life!

Key Takeaways:

Wake up every day expecting something great to happen.

Don't put limits on God because He has plans that are bigger than you can contemplate.

Great stories come from those of us willing to try, willing to get hurt, willing to look silly, and willing to succeed.

There is no "perfect time" to do something; the time to take action is NOW, so start taking steps and taking risks!

Chapter 32: Your Key Takeaways and Next Steps

I'm not just a storyteller who wants to entertain you. I genuinely want to help you. That is why my books are part memoir and part self-help.

My travel series is no different.

In the first book of my travel series, *The Blind Blogger's NYC Adventures (+ How You Can Make Your Dreams Come True),* I included a chapter at the end of the book that discussed the key points I wanted my readers to remember, which were highlighted throughout the book. In this book, *The Blind Blogger's First Speaking and Signing Adventures (+ How You Can Conquer Your Fears)*, I wanted to summarize all of the key takeaways from each chapter.

Let's review those key takeaways:

1. *You should not wait until you think your story is good enough before you start sharing it!*
2. *A great editor can help you make your story shine, come alive, and transport the reader into your world!*

3. *Seize opportunities when they come your way!*

4. *Instead of making excuses, focus on finding solutions!*

5. *Use your resources to reach out for help.*

6. *Let other people be part of your story and your success!*

7. *Plan on doing fun things during "work" trips!*

8. *Always ask others for what you want and need. Remember, "If you don't ask, they can't say yes."*

9. *Wonderful and unexpected opportunities will arise, if you reach out to your social networks.*

10. *Be open and make your desire to help others genuinely apparent.*

11. *Have faith and trust in both the Lord and in people that things will always work out.*

12. *Don't rush things; take the time to meet people, have leisurely conversations, exchange emails, and build friendships.*

13. *Don't do what others think you should do; do what YOU want!*

14. *Enjoy your work and plan on having new experiences.*

15. *Do positive things with your life!*

16. *Have faith in yourself.*

17. *Invest in yourself and hire others to help you.*

18. *The more you trust in the future, the better that future will be!*
19. *Your family and friends will likely and eventually accept whatever situation you decide to put yourself in, and offer to help you, regardless of their personal feelings.*
20. *Believe in yourself and your abilities, even if they are not perfect.*
21. *Look at a bad situation and find a solution to turn it into a good one.*
22. *Remember previous times when you overcame challenging circumstances and use those memories to help you find solutions to your current problem.*
23. *Random conversations can spark creativity, ignite laughter, and lead to new friendships.*
24. *New relationships can be found everywhere, if you are open to having them.*
25. *Take every opportunity to promote yourself, your business, or your books, because you never know who might be interested!*
26. *Be sure to travel because you will meet interesting people.*
27. *Remember to have confidence in yourself when you are promoting yourself, your business, or your books.*
28. *If you are a creative entrepreneur, always carry copies of your books,*

CDs, DVDs, shirts, and any other merchandise you have with you, along with your business cards.

29. You will get better at asking for the sale, with practice.

30. God will put people in your path that you are destined to meet.

31. Have faith that things will work out.

32. Everyone has an amazing story. (Yes, everyone, including you!)

33. Admit you aren't ready, prepare like you are, and then do your best.

34. You can overcome your fears by facing them, admitting you are scared, and by telling the truth.

35. Always be your authentic self.

36. Expect the unexpected!

37. Take time to appreciate your surroundings.

38. Everything prepares you for your future, in some way.

39. Take a small step every day.

40. Find small ways to challenge yourself and improve yourself.

41. Find fun ways to learn new skills and practice them.

42. Be open to daily opportunities to grow.

43. Don't focus on your fear; focus on the mission. Think about what you are there to do and why. Then, just do it, one thing at a time. Slow yourself

down and put everything other than your next task out of your mind.

44. *Take advantage of nice weather.*

45. *Appreciate every experience because that's how memories are made.*

46. *Remember to play back your successes in the movie screen of your mind.*

47. *If you already have a goal, then take action toward achieving it.*

48. *If you don't have any goals, create some.*

49. *Change the way you see yourself, if need be.*

50. *Build genuine friendships with others and believe them when they tell you truths about yourself.*

51. *You will be surprised when something profoundly affects you.*

52. *Opportunities lie in the strangest places or circumstances.*

53. *People will invest in you and your message.*

54. *You need to advertise or mention your products and/or services on social media.*

55. *Surprises will come to you and you will inspire others.*

56. *Money is not always what is important.*

57. *Setbacks are opportunities to find solutions.*

58. *There is danger in making assumptions, so make sure to ask questions before providing a response.*
59. *Honesty and authenticity are important.*
60. *Stories influence us to take risks and actions to pursue our dreams.*
61. *Look for the positives instead of focusing on the negatives, and try to find lessons from every experience.*
62. *Remember that life is an adventure!*
63. *Your physical, mental, emotional, and spiritual health are critical to success in business or in chasing your dreams, so make sure you don't neglect yourself in any of these areas!*
64. *Don't hesitate to seek help from someone, whether you need it or not!*
65. *Take time to enjoy and appreciate the magnificence of nature.*
66. *Don't let anything stop you from going on an adventure.*
67. *Take some risks, instead of playing it safe all the time.*
68. *Dream, and dream big.*
69. *Be prepared to change your plans, if need be.*
70. *Adjusting to something new can take time.*
71. *Be grateful for your blessings and the things you take for granted.*

72. *Meeting new people can be fascinating and talking to people helps you appreciate them more.*

73. *Help others whenever you can, if you have the means to do so—and even if you don't.*

74. *Remember to take time to enjoy the little things in life, like eating, talking, and spending time with your loved ones.*

75. *Create a game to play while doing simple activities such as watching TV or movies, to intensify the fun.*

76. *Don't be afraid of trying new things, including new methods of technology, because they might end up being more beneficial to you than may realize!*

77. *We should try to recognize our annoying quirks and then eliminate them from our lives, to grow into better people.*

78. *It's important to be respectful of others.*

79. *You can mend fences and repair damaged relationships, even if you weren't the one who broke them, if you stop worrying about who caused the wreckage and simply tried to just see each other as people.*

80. *When you stay at someone else's home, offer to pitch in, whenever possible.*

81. *Some mistakes are blessings in disguise.*
82. *There are a lot of people who truly want to and will help you.*
83. *Be open to changing your hair and/or clothing style, because it may be just the improvement you need to look more successful!*
84. *Even though looks are not everything, having an improved look will help you feel better.*
85. *When you have good company, good weather, and good money, it's easy to be happy.*
86. *Remember your loved ones and take time to reminisce because good memories will also make you happy.*
87. *Don't be so focused on your mission that you miss out on some great experience.*
88. *Take time to enjoy every experience.*
89. *We sometimes need to relearn important lessons.*
90. *Live life as if everything is an experience to be treasured.*
91. *Having comfortable shoes on your feet is vital to good health as well as your success.*
92. *Wake up every day expecting something great to happen.*
93. *Don't put limits on God because He has plans that are bigger than you can contemplate.*

94. *Great stories come from those of us willing to try, willing to get hurt, willing to look silly, and willing to succeed.*
95. *There is no "perfect time" to do something; the time to take action is NOW, so start taking steps and taking risks!*

While many of these key takeaways don't specifically mention the word "fear," it is important to note that these pieces of advice all relate to helping you conquer your fears, whatever your fears might be.

Your next steps, then, are to implement these takeaways into your life and your daily practices. If you need help, I'm here for you. Just email me or send me a message on social media. I sincerely want you to succeed in your endeavors and will help you in any way that I can.

Everything starts by taking one small step. Don't wait any longer. Go take your step now!

A Special Note from the Author

This is the part where I acknowledge all the people who contributed to the book or helped with the journey.

I want to start by remembering four awesome people who have passed on since the events in this book occurred.

First up is my cousin, Judy Cory, who doesn't figure directly in this book, but she helped me immeasurably during my Amtrak adventure to New York City. She contributed money, reassured my mom that I would be okay, and encouraged me to just go for it. She was always supportive of me, whether it was regarding my ability to sell amusement equipment or to travel the country. She was a very classy lady who was always there. Judy died from lung cancer, which she fought with the same positive outlook that she encouraged me to live my life with. Without her help, there may not have been a first trip, much less a continuing series of adventures.

Next up is my Aunt Francis. She was a feisty lady when I first met her, and I could still feel her spirit when I saw her during my trip. She may have been small in stature, but she still had a vibrancy to her—something that I think is genetic to the Ivey women. Aunt Francis lived past eighty years old and was surrounded by four generations of her family when she passed away. I'll miss her zest for life.

Then there is Mark Gardner, Paula's husband—a hardworking, God-fearing, family man who believed in enjoying the simple pleasures of life. He loved his family, NASCAR, the beach, the lake, concerts, and having a good meal. I enjoyed seeing him with his kids. He was a really loving dad. Mark welcomed me into his home and made me feel welcome. I know people talk about southern hospitality, and they wonder if such a thing still exists. Well, Mark did us Southerners proud. He died from a massive heart attack. But unlike some people who work themselves to death, he enjoyed life, to the fullest. He and Paula were out on a date, having a nice meal, before going to a concert they wanted to see. To show how perfect he and Paula were, she continues to live a fulfilled life now. I have no doubt that she would be willing to go on my next adventure—providing it doesn't come during the school year.

Finally, there is my Uncle Vernon. I'm not sure whether he is Vernon III or IV, but he gave me some great memories. He shared stories of my dad, Maxwell Ivey, Sr., and told me I took after him. He encouraged me to sing, even if I don't know the words. He worked outdoors in construction for years and contracted skin cancer. It migrated to other parts of his body. Eventually, he succumbed.

Next, I want to thank the other people who took me into their homes or gave me opportunities.

The first one is Joe (Super Joe) Pardo. When I met him by appearing on his podcast, I had no idea how much of an impact he was going to have on my life. That one conversation led me to speaking at DreamCon and again at his signature event, Indie Pod Con. I met Chris Krimitsos, Staci Greenberg, Karen Yankovich, Azuka Zuke, Erica Blocker, Chip Edwards, and so many more through Joe, his events, and his community. He gave a first-time speaker the mic, even though he probably didn't know how the heck this blind guy was going to get to Philadelphia, much less what kind of speaker I would be. He had faith. I also want to thank him for writing the foreword for this book.

Then there was Al Chase and Deb Basil. Al only knew me from Facebook, and Deb didn't know me at all, yet they took me into their home, fed me, washed my clothes, took me places, and shared themselves with me.

Then there is Michael, Michele, and their family. Our previous time together in the carnival business hadn't been fun because we were living in a stressful situation with a constant lack of money. When I asked about visiting them during this speaking and signing trip, they had no way of knowing if I had changed for the better. I'm truly appreciative of the fact that Michele said "YES" before I even heard from Michael.

Next up is Paula, Mark, and their family.

Paula and Mark not only gave me a place to stay, but they truly welcomed me—which is how I believe family members *should* treat each other. It's comforting to know that no matter how long it's been since you saw each other last, you will always find a warm welcome, a good meal, and some great hugs.

I want to thank Amtrak and their staff, even though they will probably never realize how much they continue to figure in my story. I keep hoping they will decide to sponsor me, my podcast, and my future journey. I wouldn't have gone on my first big adventure without them or their contest. That one trip to New York City has led me to have the belief that I can go off on even bigger, scarier, more daunting trips.

I also want to say thanks, in general, to all the great people I met while traveling on

Amtrak—from the people who I had conversations with (who are mentioned in this book) to the many staff members who went out of their way, to ensure I got where I needed to be. Because of their team, I never felt like I was at risk in any way, while getting from one destination to another.

I also want to thank my family, who lives here, in Houston: Patrick, Seth, and my mom.

My brother, Patrick, works nights, stocking shelves at Walmart, to help pay the bills, so I don't have to feel the pressure of supporting the family all by myself. He is never slow in offering to help me take that next trip.

My nephew, Seth, used to think I couldn't go anywhere without him or without someone else going with me. Seth now helps out a lot, whenever I'm preparing for my next trip. He also learned from Chelsea C. Nguyen (who will be mentioned in my next book!) how to cut and dye my hair. I can always depend on Seth to buy me good snacks for the road, too.

My mom, who is currently 76, will always worry about me. She wants her kids here, with her, where it's safe, even if she sometimes admits that it's not really safe anywhere. I have noticed that once I leave for my trips, she is the most encouraging while I'm gone. She's not a big Facebook user, but she follows all my posts. She even started asking me to send photos and videos directly to her iPhone, so she can see them earlier and share them herself! That way, she gets to brag about her kid to the rest of the family.

Finally, I want to thank all of the people who have been following my progress. Knowing you are watching and being inspired by my exploits fuels my determination to keep going. It challenges me to take on more and share more. It reminds me that on days when I don't feel like showing up, I'll disappoint my fans and supporters, if I fail to do so.

Without my friends, fans, and followers, I would have a lot harder of a time doing all that I do. I hope you realize that, appreciate it, and give yourself some of the credit for it. I couldn't do this without you. (Okay, maybe I could, but it wouldn't be as much fun or as satisfying.) I can't wait to start telling you about my future travel adventures.

I have at least two more books in this travel series, from past experiences, that I want to finish, publish, and share.

I need to take advantage of the pandemic's "stay in place" orders, to get them down on paper.

Before I end, I have to thank Lorraine Reguly, who is amazingly talented and incredibly patient. She has helped me bring my books to life, through editing, formatting, and all of the other steps of the publication process. She's more than just my editor.

Lorraine is a friend who has supported me since we met in 2013. She also serves as "my eyes," and is the person who had to make the design decisions for the book covers in this series.

I also have to thank the graphics artist she worked with, Ravi Verma, who helped bring Lorraine's vision for the covers into existence.

Ravi did an excellent job and always meets the guidelines that Amazon/KDP set out for the cover sizes and specifications. Lorraine's job in working with Ravi and then describing to me, in detail, what my book covers look like couldn't have been easy! Thank you both, once again!

Thank you, everyone, again, too, for your part in my stories. I look forward to having you along on my next big adventures!

About the Author

Born into a family of carnival owners in Texas, USA, Maxwell Ivey was diagnosed with Retinitis Pigmentosa (RP) and started losing his sight at age 12. Having a natural gusto for life, Max became heavily involved in the Scouts, achieving the rank of Eagle Scout. By the time he graduated from college, he was completely blind. He also worked in the family business alongside his brothers until his father succumbed to lung cancer.

Faced with his own mortality, Max made some life-altering changes.

He underwent gastric surgery and lost over 250 pounds. He started his own business, buying and selling amusement rides, and learned how to blog using software for visually-impaired people.

Overcoming many obstacles, Max made a name for himself online and now shares his experiences as The Blind Blogger, on the website that shares this name.

Max's favourite things entail teaching and helping others achieve their goals.

Max now spends his days singing, reading, blogging, speaking, writing, creating videos, coaching, and podcasting. Max is the host of the "What's Your Excuse? Show."

Max would like to travel the world one day and meet his many online friends and clients in person. He'd also like to meet a special lady to share his life with.

Max can be found on social media, too, so please connect with him on:

1: Facebook at
https://www.facebook.com/Mr.Midway

2: LinkedIn at
https://www.linkedin.com/in/maxwellivey

3: Twitter using @maxwellivey or
https://twitter.com/maxwellivey

4: The Midway Marketplace at
http://midwaymarketplace.com/

To stay updated and be notified when other books are released, please visit The Blind Blogger at http://theblindblogger.net/ and sign up to Max's email list!

About *Leading You Out of the Darkness into the Light*

Maxwell's Ivey's debut book is a motivational book in which Max shares the 11 steps of his success as a blind entrepreneur and the lessons he has learned from his journey. It also provides 11 exercises for readers to do, complete with email support from the author.

It is Max's sincerest desire to help you succeed in accomplishing your goals or achieving your dreams! Stop the excuses and get started on your success journey today!

If you purchase this book from Selz (which enables Max to earn a higher royalty percentage), you'll get 1 PDF, 11 specific steps to follow, and 11 specific, actionable exercises to complete. Purchase it via https://maxwellivey.selz.com/.

You can also purchase it in e-book or print format from Amazon.

Regardless of where you buy this book, throughout it all, Max will be with you, guiding you, helping you, and offering you his support.

This is more than just a book. It's a chance to change your life!

About *It's Not the Cookie, It's the Bag: An Easy-to-Follow Guide for Weight Loss Success*

Everyone knows that changing your lifestyle is not easy.

Whether you are trying to lose weight or trying to keep it off, you need an action plan you can follow. The thing is... it doesn't have to be hard. It can be fun, simple, and easy!

In *It's Not the Cookie, It's the Bag*, blind man Maxwell Ivey Jr shares the ups and downs of his weight loss—and weight maintenance—journey to good health.

He also reveals **the exact methods** he uses in his day-to-day life to achieve and maintain his phenomenal success.

Going from 512 pounds to a 250-pound, lean, mean machine in just two years, Max tells you how YOU can replicate his success and become the person you *want* to be... the person you were *meant* to be... the person you *deserve* to be... one small step at a time.

So what are you waiting for?

Get started today!

Use Max's methods to become happy for the rest of your life!

After all, if a blind man can do this, why can't you?

If you purchase this book from Selz via https://maxwellivey.selz.com/, it will enable Max to earn a higher royalty percentage.

You can also purchase it in e-book or print format from Amazon.

About *The Blind Blogger's NYC Adventures (+ How You Can Make YOUR Dreams Come True)*

This is the true story of Maxwell Ivey and his adventures in New York City.

It contains many life lessons and explains how you can make your dreams come true, using the keys to success Max regularly uses to attain his own goals and make his dreams a reality.

Max is a blind entrepreneur, blogger, author, and podcaster. He won Amtrak's 2016 prestigious Writers in Residency Award, which included a trip to any city in the USA. He chose to travel to NYC... alone! He chronicled each of his adventures, which include being on a TV show, going ice-skating in Rockefeller Center, meeting the Blogger from Paradise in person... and more!

Max displays a remarkable amount of courage and willingness to chase his dreams, despite the obstacles in his way. He is a great role model who teaches others how they can work towards their dreams and ultimately reach them... no matter what.

Using creative narration, accompanying photos, and funny stories, Max also makes the readers laugh with his witticisms about being blind... as in the case of sitting backwards on the train, because the scenery is the same regardless of which way he is facing.

This is Max's first book in his travel series. Read it. Enjoy it. Learn from it. And become armed with the secrets to achieving your own dreams, too!

Buy *The Blind Blogger's NYC Adventures* on Selz or buy it on Amazon (in print or as an e-book). If you purchase this book from Selz via https://maxwellivey.selz.com/, it will enable Max to earn a higher royalty percentage.

About *The Blind Blogger's First Speaking and Signing Adventures (+ How You Can Conquer Your Fears)*

This is the second book in Max's travel series. Max has since travelled to other places, and is working on more books!

To stay updated and be notified when other books in this series are released, please visit http://theblindblogger.net and sign up to Max's email list!

Upcoming Books

Max has plans for at least two more books in his travel series. To stay updated and be notified when other books in this series are released, please visit The Blind Blogger at http://theblindblogger.net and sign up to Max's email list!

Made in the USA
Middletown, DE
20 November 2025

22217917R00146